Y GREB · JACK DEMPSEY · BENNY LEONAR
LOUIS · SUGAR RAY ROBINSON · WILLIE
ORGE FOREMAN · SUGAR RAY LEONARD ·
· HARRY GREB · JACK DEMPSEY · BENNY
OORE · JOE LOUIS · SUGAR RAY ROBINSO
MAD ALI · GEORGE FOREMAN · SUGAR RA
· JACK JOHNSON · HARRY GREB · JACK
TRONG · ARCHIE MOORE · JOE LOUIS · SU
IANO · MUHAMMAD ALI · GEORGE FOREM
L. SULLIVAN · JACK JOHNSON · HARRY
ARMSTRONG · ARCHIE MOORE · JOE LOU
KY MARCIANO · MUHAMMAD ALI · GEOR
ON · JOHN L. SULLIVAN · JACK JOHNSON
ARD · HENRY ARMSTRONG · ARCHIE MO
E PEP · ROCKY MARCIANO · MUHAMMAD
RD · MIKE TYSON · JOH LLIVAN ·
BENNY LEONARD · HEN ONG ·
OBINSON · WILLIE PEP · ROCK ARCIAN
GAR RAY LEONARD · MIKE TYSON · JOHN
JACK DEMPSEY · BENNY LEONARD · HEN
SUGAR RAY ROBINSON · WILLIE PEP · R

Rocky Marciano
WORLD'S HEAVYWEIGHT CHAMPION
MGR. AL WEILL

The IMMORTALS *of* American Boxing

Sonny
Liston

The IMMORTALS of American Boxing

Don Stradley

GELDING STREET PRESS

A Gelding Street Press book
An imprint of Rockpool Publishing
PO Box 252
Summer Hill
NSW 2130 Australia

geldingstreetpress.com
Follow us! @ Geldingstreetpress

ISBN: 9781922662279

Published in 2025 by Gelding Street Press

Design and typesetting by Christine Armstrong, Rockpool Publishing
Edited by Brooke Halliwell

A catalogue record for this book is available from the National Library of Australia

Printed and bound in China

10 9 8 7 6 5 4 3 2 1

Front cover & p. ii: Muhammad Ali stands over Sonny Liston, round one, Lewiston, Maine, 1965.
Back cover: Jack Dempsey (right) versus Georges Carpentier, 1921.

DEDICATION

In memory of Bert Sugar (1936–2012), an author, curmudgeon, and friend. We once talked about writing a book together. And to whoever stocked the magazine rack at Fernandes Supermarket when I was a boy in Brockton. It was always full of boxing magazines. I'd place one discreetly in my mother's shopping cart. And to my mother. She never minded buying me an issue of *The Ring* which, at the time, was edited by Bert Sugar.

Sugar Ray Leonard pummels Thomas Hearns in their second bout, 1989.

Contents

Jack Dempsey showing how a boxing Immortal should look.

Introduction

When Gelding Street Press approached me to write a book called *The Immortals of American Boxing*, my mind started to race.

I've written about boxing for many years, mostly for *The Ring* magazine. Trust me, the easiest way to rile boxing fans is to present a list. My task was to choose 15 American fighters to be dubbed "Immortal." Fortunately, I didn't have to rank them in terms of importance. I had only to present them chronologically and tell their stories. Yet the idea of selecting 15 fighters was daunting.

How far back did I want to go? Bareknuckle days? Should such miscreants as Kid McCoy and Abe Attell be considered? For that matter, how many contemporary names did I want on the list? And what makes an Immortal, anyway?

In a previous book from Gelding Street Press, *The Immortals of Australian Surfing*, author Phil Jarratt claimed his choices were "individuals whose fame and feats are expected to endure forever." I wasn't sure how many fighters could meet that standard. America's attention span being what it is, some of this country's greatest fighters were forgotten in their own lifetimes. Yet the assignment intrigued me.

As I pondered the hundreds of great American fighters, I hashed out my criteria.

A fighter's win-loss record would play only a minor part in my choices. Records are interesting, but deceptive. For one thing, record keeping was inexact in the pioneer days of boxing. The records of old-time fighters are difficult to verify. Moreover, modern fighters can achieve an impressive record thanks to careful matchmaking. Many great fighters from a century ago lost fights early in their career, which is less likely now because modern fighters are brought along so carefully. To me, a fighter's win-loss record is worth pondering, but greatness is usually down to how he performs in a few important fights.

All of the fighters chosen for this book are enshrined in the International Boxing Hall of Fame in Canastota, New York. Most were inducted as part of the 1990 inaugural class. Yet Hall of Fame credentials didn't count for much regarding this book. Many fighters are honored in the Hall but, despite what the venue's organizers would say, they're not all Immortals.

Pure boxing skill was certainly considered, though geniuses such as Tommy Loughran and Pernell Whitaker didn't make the list. Sheer toughness wasn't enough either. That's why I could find no room for Tony Zale, Carmen Basilio, and a few dozen other hard guys. Popularity was a factor, though Ray "Boom Boom" Mancini, one of the most recognized household names of the 1980s, is nowhere near the list.

I trod lightly in the era of "no-decision" contests. This was roughly between 1910 and 1925, when bouts fought in certain states were arranged so that unless there was a knockout, there would be no winner. Newspapers would report that one man might've dominated the action, hence the phrase "newspaper decision," but the contests would go onto a fighter's record as "ND." This was designed to curtail gambling and to prevent arguments over the verdict, but the rule had a negative effect on the business. Champions could take part in no-decision bouts, look terrible, and keep their title. Many ND bouts were glorified exhibitions. Jack Britton had 187 ND bouts, and with all due respect to "The Boxing Marvel," I doubt he was going for broke in all of them. Yet the ND era produced Benny Leonard and Harry Greb, two surefire Immortals.

Instinct also told me to stay out of the recent era. I couldn't imagine bumping Greb to make room for Floyd Mayweather Jr. or Oscar De La Hoya. Floyd and Oscar were major modern attractions, but it's too soon to think of them as Immortals. For that matter, American society has changed, and so has boxing's place in it. There was a time when no sports figure was as important as the heavyweight champion, a time when the president would call a new champion and congratulate him on his victory. This is no longer true.

Ultimately, my selections hinged on two factors.

First, they had to be trailblazers. Henry Armstrong being the only man to win three titles simultaneously is a case in point, or Jack Johnson being the first Black heavyweight champion. Second, the fighters had to penetrate the culture in some way. Think Joe Louis. Think Muhammad Ali.

Once I selected my 15 Immortals, I was struck by the similarity of their stories. For instance, almost all of them experienced the public turning against them. Also, many of these fighters spent some time away from the business and made dramatic comebacks. And is it just a coincidence that most of them had stormy personal lives? It seemed the excitement of the ring and their level of stardom could only be matched by reckless living.

The connecting through-line, however, was what these fighters meant to the American people. There's a kind of monotheism in boxing – the public usually goes for one fighter in a big way. And beating him doesn't mean you replace him in the public eye. In 2004 a fellow named Danny Williams defeated Mike Tyson, but Tyson remained the star, and Williams remained a hardworking journeyman. The public decides these things.

Dempsey floors Georges Carpentier. Jersey City, 1921.

And in a way, though I'm pleased with my selections, the public had declared these fighters Immortal long ago.

Don Stradley

John L. Sullivan in his prime. 1882.

John L. Sullivan

Full name:	John Lawrence Sullivan
Nickname:	The Boston Strong Boy
Birthdate:	October 15, 1858; died February 2, 1918
Place of birth:	Boston, Massachusetts

He was crude and scandalous, but he took prizefighting out of the wastelands and gave it mass appeal.

Modern boxing begins with John L. Sullivan in 1880s America. No other figure was as influential on the business of fighting. It is generally believed that his brash personality caused the breakthrough, but his oversized image would've meant nothing if not for his aggressive style in the ring. Sullivan didn't merely defeat opponents. He trampled over them.

In many ways, Sullivan's career was the template that many great fighters would appear to follow long after his death in 1918. Whether they were shamelessly bragging, going into show business, wasting their fortunes, or offending the public with bad behavior, no future champion would go where Sullivan hadn't already been. He was also the prototype for those who ended up as pitiable wrecks, for his eventual downfall was just as dramatic as his spectacular rise.

Sullivan claimed the heavyweight championship of America by defeating Paddy Ryan in Mississippi City on February 7, 1882. The event took place at a time when the London Prize Ring Rules were being supplanted by the more orderly Marquess of Queensberry Rules. London Rules involved bare knuckles and grappling; a round was called when a fighter was thrown, knocked down, or deliberately dropped to the ground, which meant a round could last one minute or 10. A fallen fighter had 30 seconds to recover. The Queensberry Rules called for three-minute rounds with 60-second breaks, no grappling, and a bit more civility. A downed fighter had 10 seconds to rise. The newer guidelines also required the combatants to wear small gloves.

Sullivan favored the Queensberry system, but to compete for the title he agreed to the knockabout, bare-fisted mayhem preferred by Ryan. Yet the rules were unimportant. Sullivan was 23 and as fit as a lion. Ryan was near 30 and reportedly weakened by a recent illness.

The makeshift ring had been pitched on the lawn of the Barnes Hotel next to an oak grove. Approximately 2,000 spectators witnessed the event. Some perched in the trees, while others crowded the hotel balcony, all wondering if the police would intervene. Prizefighting was illegal in America, giving the affair a distinctly outlaw feel. The criminal atmosphere was magnified by rumors that the notorious bandits, Frank and Jesse James, were somewhere in the gathering.

Sources differ on the actual length of the bout, but it ended when Sullivan drove his right fist into Ryan's neck, under the left ear. Ryan crumpled and couldn't continue. According to the *Baltimore Sun*, Sullivan bounded out of the ring without a mark on him, "running to his quarters at a lively gait and laughing." The new champion knew the good times were about to begin.

There'd been some well-known fighters in previous decades, but stateside interest had waned. Upon the emergence of Sullivan, however, prizefighting roared to life in America. With his outsized persona, Sullivan fit perfectly alongside the mythical sharpshooters and lumberjacks who had become the country's folk heroes. But he needed no rifle or axe. All he needed was his massive fist. "It felt," Ryan said, "like a telegraph pole had been shoved against me endways."

He was born October 15, 1858, in Boston's South End, an Irish neighborhood in a city known

Sullivan, showing the effects of alcohol and high living.

then as "the Dublin of America." Though the Irish American populace was notably poor in that time and place, and often suffered the indignities of racism,

"If you want to know what it is to be struck by lightning, just face Sullivan for one second."

Sullivan was not impoverished and was reasonably educated. Legend has it that he was considering a career in baseball, or perhaps the priesthood. Yet even as a teenager he was impressing people with feats of strength and settling arguments with his fists. Unable to keep a job because of his aggressive nature, and unimpressed with local pugilists he saw in Boston athletic clubs, he decided at 19 to enter the frowned upon business of prizefighting.

He quickly developed a reputation in the eastern states, defeating rivals in remote venues – a derelict barroom in Cincinnati, a barge anchored in the Hudson River – any grim location unknown to local constables. Sullivan was swift and strong, and unlike the older breed of fighters who liked to wear opponents down over a long contest, he usually sprinted from his corner and ended things quickly. As one of his unfortunate victims pointed out, "If you want to know

Sullivan (left) moves in on Jake Kilrain. Richburg, Mississippi, 1889.

what it is to be struck by lightning, just face Sullivan for one second."

Reporters often described him as a "colossus," or "Herculean," while newspaper cartoonists depicted him as a strutting giant surrounded by Lilliputian admirers. In fact, Sullivan was listed at 5'10", and in his fighting prime weighed around 200 pounds. He was no giant, but Sullivan was certainly larger than the average man of his time. Rare photos of Sullivan in 1882 show a husky young man with dark, angry eyes, and thick arms seemingly designed for punching. His famous handlebar mustache came later but would become a fixed part of the Sullivan image, that of the mustachioed Irish brawler. Yet Sullivan was surprisingly boyish in those early photographs, like a callow farm boy dressed in his Sunday finest. Undoubtedly, it was Sullivan's youthful appearance that inspired his long-lasting nickname, "The Boston Strong Boy."

Sullivan had the flair of a natural showman, assuring his admirers that he could "lick any son of a bitch in the house." He was vulgar, but as America was growing into a world power, Sullivan embodied the young country's exuberance, its desire for recognition. By 1881 a simple exhibition he gave at the New York Aquarium drew nearly 1,500 paying customers. Another 1,000 purportedly lingered outside and watched through the windows. This was unheard of for a mere sparring session, but the public was curious about this new fistic phenomenon. Irish Americans, still shamed by signs in storefronts reading "No Irish Need Apply," saw Sullivan as a beacon.

Some journalists dismissed the craze for Sullivan as a temporary fad, but the crowds only grew once he became champion. A crowd of 10,000 jammed Madison Square Garden in 1883 to watch Sullivan battle Herbert Slade, the Māori Giant. In a gloved contest to differentiate it from the still illegal bareknuckle style, Sullivan stopped Slade in three rounds. Yet the action seemed less newsworthy than the horde that had assembled to observe the champion at work. Along with the usual crowd of criminals and roughnecks, the United Press noted the throng included "judges, senators and politicians of all grades, bankers and brokers, and sporting men of all classes." It appeared Sullivan had done more than commercialize prizefighting. He'd gentrified it.

Two key factors aided Sullivan's rise to fame. The invention of the telegraph, for instance, sent news of his antics all around the country, with spectacular crowds gathering at newspaper offices hoping for the latest dispatch about his fights. Moreover, his favoring of gloves allowed Sullivan to make more ring appearances. Unlike bareknuckle fighters who fought infrequently because of the illicitness of their business, Sullivan could wear "the pillows" and put on regular exhibitions where and when he pleased.

Like a modern-day rock star hitting the road, Sullivan and a group of sparring partners traveled to music halls and theaters across America on what he called his "Knocker-out Tours." The events were advertised loudly in newspapers as if a circus were coming, heralded as "The Great John L. Sullivan Combination," or "Sullivan's Sluggers." The programs could include anything from sparring exhibitions to demonstrations of the latest exercise equipment. (Indeed, Sullivan's camp is usually credited with the invention of the punching bag, conceived by hanging a football from a rope so Sullivan could practice hitting it.) At the climax of the evening, Sullivan would appear onstage and address the audience.

What the customers saw was an impressive figure of a man in emerald-green tights, brown fighting boots, and baggy white sweater, looking every bit the gladiator that had been described by journalists. Finally, Americans from the farms and coalmines were going to witness a real boxer in action. But when Sullivan began moving around with a sparring partner, he seemed to be playing. His hands, encased in large white mitts, moved artfully

He made noises as he fought, bellowing like a mad beast in the wilderness.

enough, but he was working at half-speed. Spectators might've jeered, but this was part of Sullivan's game.

Sullivan had made the tour more intriguing with an offer of money, sometimes as much as $1,000, to anyone who could last four rounds with him. Inevitably some railroader or local strong man would take up the challenge and approach the stage. The audience would hold its breath as the real fighting began. Now Sullivan was serious. He made noises as he fought, bellowing like a mad beast in the wilderness. The legend now had breadth and dimension, color and sound. On most nights Sullivan needed only a few blows to send his challenger hurtling into the orchestra pit.

The evening always ended with Sullivan's ready-made farewell speech, thanking the "wonderful people" for coming out: "I plan to remain the champion of America for as long as I'm able to raise a fist. I remain your good friend, as always, John L. Sullivan."

Though mythmakers may have inflated the numbers, it was believed Sullivan defeated 50 challengers on the 1883 tour, and an additional 29 during a second junket that stretched into 1884. Other tours followed, including a jubilant trip to England where the Prince of Wales attended one of Sullivan's programs. "He's a marvel of a man," said the prince, "altogether out of the ordinary."

But even as he grew into a fabled figure, Sullivan was often involved in scandals. There was a very public divorce where Sullivan's wife accused him of abusing her. He'd blatantly taken on a mistress who traveled with him, a chorus line dancer named Ann Livingston. When his young son died of diphtheria, Sullivan skipped the funeral because he was on tour. As the bad press mounted, the debauched and wicked champion continued zigzagging across the nation, throwing dollar bills out of hotel windows to the crowds below.

Sullivan's abuse of alcohol was also out of control. His weary entourage was tasked with bringing him to engagements on time and keeping him sober, jobs for which they were grossly underpaid.

Somehow, even as his drinking increased, Sullivan remained the heavyweight champion for a decade. His bouts took on an epic quality, particularly a three-hour draw in 1888 with Charlie Mitchell in Chantilly, France, fought bareknuckle on muddy turf as rain poured down.

The zenith of Sullivan's reign was a grueling bout with Jake Kilrain in 1889, fought under London Rules in Richburg, Mississippi. Kilrain surrendered after the 75th round. It had been far from glamorous – at one point Sullivan vomited in the ring – but it would be remembered as the champion's most impressive victory. Historically it was considered the official end of bareknuckle fights in America, but the real story was Sullivan's endurance. He'd lasted more than two hours in the punishing Mississippi heat. *The Boston Globe* suggested the Seven

Wonders of the World be expanded to eight, with the inclusion of the city's notorious champion.

By now Sullivan's star was higher than ever. He'd inspired a popular song, "Let Me Shake the Hand that Shook the Hand of Sullivan." He owned a popular saloon in Boston. He embarked on an acting career, touring in a play called *Honest Hearts and Willing Hands*. However, the country's greatest battler was tired of fighting. Training for Kilrain had been a miserable experience for him, compounded by stomach ailments and mysterious fevers, while the bout's aftermath saw Sullivan spend a fortune in legal fees to keep himself out of prison for prizefighting.

While Sullivan amused himself outside of boxing, a few suitable challengers emerged. One, a Black fighter out of Australia named Peter Jackson, was snubbed because Sullivan refused to fight non-whites. Sullivan wore his bigotry like a badge, but it was complex. He counted among his friends the great Black bantamweight, George Dixon. Yet when it came to challengers, Sullivan drew the "color line." Some biographers have claimed Sullivan simply reflected the racist attitudes of his day, while others suggest he was showing solidarity with his Irish American admirers, a group suddenly competing against Black Americans for jobs after the Civil War.

It could also have been that Sullivan, in his ragged state, didn't think he could beat Jackson. He may have felt his devotees would rather hear he was a racist than lacking confidence. Regardless, Jackson was matched against the other top challenger of the era, James J. Corbett of San Francisco. They battled for 61 rounds to a draw. Sullivan, looking for a payday in between acting jobs, saw Corbett as a possible challenger.

In September of 1892, a graying and overweight Sullivan faced Corbett at the New Orleans Olympic Club, a sparkling modern venue fitted with electric lights. With advances in newswire technology and the benefit of a long buildup, it was the biggest sporting event of the age. Fought under the Queensberry Rules with gloves, it showed how boxing had become a regulated, highly commercial business. Yet it was a disaster for the reigning champion. Corbett, a scientific young boxer known as "Gentleman Jim," knocked Sullivan out in the 21st round. Hours after his humiliating defeat, the ex-champion was seen weeping with his handlers. "Since Napoleon stood on the bleak rock of St. Helena and thought of Austerlitz," wrote the *Brooklyn Daily Eagle*, "there has been no spectacle more touching than that of the beaten prizefighter, crying from the bottom of his heart, 'John L. is a goner.'"

Sullivan's title was gone but his popularity endured. A riot erupted on his return to Boston, as thousands crammed into the Park Street Depot, flattening a police barricade to welcome "Sully" home. Pushing his way through the crowd, Sullivan boarded an awaiting carriage that was to bring him to his sister's house. A few hundred men and boys surrounded the carriage and ran alongside it for nearly a mile, shouting and waving their hats. To his admirers, Sullivan hadn't lost to Corbett. He'd lost to the bottle.

The Great John L. as elder statesman.

While Sullivan's popularity was secure, the same couldn't be said for his official ring record. Historians have argued for more than a century over which of his bouts should be counted, and whether his bareknuckle wins should be included with his bouts fought under Queensberry Rules. The

Sullivan often invited admirers to, "Shake the hand that shook the world."

most recently accepted stats on him are 47-1-2, with 38 wins by knockout. His tours would've earned him another 100 or more "unofficial" wins.

Sullivan's middle years were bleak. He remained a public figure, yet he sometimes seemed like a ghost of pugilism's past, sick, broke, and pathetic.

In 1905, at age 46 and as hefty as a porpoise, Sullivan donned the mitts one last time and KO'd 26-year-old Jim McCormick in two rounds. The crowd in Grand Rapids, Michigan, erupted as Sullivan landed a thundering blow to McCormick's jaw and left him unconscious for 10 minutes. The event spurred talk of a comeback, but Sullivan knew better.

He reinvented himself as a sort of temperance speaker, visiting more than 100 cities to preach against the evils of alcohol. Even as a teetotaler, Sullivan often invited admirers to, "Shake the hand that shook the world."

Sullivan seemed at peace during his final years. He married a childhood sweetheart, Kate Harkins, purchased a farm in Abington, Massachusetts, and adopted a son. In the winter of 1918, John L. agreed to appear with The Ringling Brothers Circus. Those plans were quashed when he died of heart failure at 59. Police found $15.00 under his pillow, supposedly all that remained of the fortune he'd earned. The ground at the Calvary Cemetery in Roslindale was frozen on the day of his burial and had to be dynamited. To the very end, Sullivan was making a loud noise.

It became common to dismiss Sullivan as a relic, a man whose legend was no more vital than an old top hat behind museum glass. He was part of the past, a time when America had only 38 states. Subsequent generations of Irish Americans no longer sought inspiration from him, for the days of two-hour fights under the blazing Mississippi sun seemed like the stuff of fiction. Additionally, his reputation as a bigot hurt him, as did the fact that most photographs of Sullivan showed him as an older man, bloated by alcohol, not the stout figure of the 1880s but a sort of melancholy walrus.

Yet his impact on boxing was immense and undeniable. His absolute patriotism had something to do with it, for Sullivan was always a proud American. And, for all of his shortcomings, there was something about him that moved people. He provided Americans with an image of what they wanted to be – tough, honest, hardheaded, crude, perhaps, and imperfect, but impossible to ignore. No other fighter from that time could've popularized boxing as Sullivan did. But he was more than just the right man at the right moment. With his awesome power, comical arrogance, and very human failings, it was as if he'd sprung directly from the country's imagination, answering some collective need for a man both triumphant and flawed.

John L. Sullivan Statistics	
Heavyweight Champion (London Rules)	1882–1889
Heavyweight Champion (Queensberry Rules)	1885–1892
Wins	47
KOs	38
Losses	1
Draws	2
No-contests	1
Total bouts	51

Jack Johnson, one of the most controversial boxing champions of all time.

2

JACK JOHNSON

Full name:	John Arthur Johnson
Nickname:	The Galveston Giant, The Golden Smile
Birthdate:	March 31, 1878; died June 10, 1946
Place of birth:	Galveston, Texas

He attracted controversy, but Jack Johnson was determined to do things his way.

On the morning after Christmas, 1908, approximately 20,000 spectators filled up a temporary stadium in Rushcutters Bay in Sydney, Australia. They'd come to witness the world heavyweight boxing champion, Tommy Burns, defend the title against Jack Johnson. With Burns being a white man from Canada and Johnson a Black man from America, the contest was significant. A victory by Johnson would make him the first Black heavyweight champion.

The implication of this was profound, especially in America where the days of slavery ended a mere 43 years earlier. Black fighters had won titles in the lighter weight classes, but the heavyweight championship had been the exclusive domain of white fighters. It was the most important title in all of sports, and to white boxing enthusiasts it represented a kind of supremacy. John L. Sullivan had set the standard. None of the champions who followed him – James J. Corbett, Bob Fitzsimmons, James J. Jeffries, Marvin Hart, and certainly not Burns – could match Sullivan's popularity, but they continued the tradition of white fighters ruling boxing's

A dramatic moment from the 15th and final round of Johnson's bout with James J. Jeffries. Reno, Nevada, 1910.

premier weight class. So important was this white idea of superiority that some believed Burns had only agreed to fight a "negro" because the event was rigged for him to win. Johnson, however, punched holes in that theory.

Johnson knocked Burns down in the bout's first minute and then toyed with him for the remainder of a one-sided contest. It seemed unfair; at six-feet tall, Johnson was much taller than Burns, and at 198 outweighed him by 30 or more pounds. The fight was so easy for Johnson that he occasionally turned to the spectators and taunted them with flashes of his gold teeth.

> News of Johnson's victory crackled like an electric current throughout America's Black communities.

Johnson had been denied a title shot for years because he was Black. It was only when promoter Hugh McIntosh offered Burns $30,000, the largest sum ever offered to a boxer to that time, that the fight was made. Yet the contest was so uneven that police jumped into the ring in round 14 and ordered McIntosh to stop the event. Burns was finished. The new champion was a Black man.

Within days, American newspapers were full of stories bemoaning the title change. The displeasure was subtle at first. Writers praised Johnson for his obvious talent as a fighter, yet the kudos was usually qualified with disparaging comments about Burns. Many claimed he was too small to be a heavyweight and was nothing more than a money-grabbing impostor. Praise for Johnson came with the caveat that he'd simply been too large for the greedy little Canuck. Johnson, in turn, teased the press. "I could've put him away quicker," he said, "but I wanted to punish him."

News of Johnson's victory crackled like an electric current throughout America's Black communities. Celebrations went on for days. Black leaders declared that Johnson's triumph in Australia was a sign of things to come for the Black race in America.

For his part, Johnson was less interested in advancing his people than he was in advancing himself. His priorities were money, women, and lively times. At the age of 30 he'd achieved his goal of becoming heavyweight champion. The reign of Jack Johnson, however, would be uneasy.

Johnson was born March 31, 1878, in Galveston, Texas. His father was a school janitor. His mother looked after Johnson and his siblings. Johnson's upbringing was typical for the first Black generation born after slavery. As a teen he worked menial jobs and spent his afternoons gambling. He also showed a talent for fighting.

Prizefighting was illegal in Texas, but Johnson developed a minor reputation in bootleg fights. It's also believed he took part in battle royals, contests where several Black youths were placed in a ring, sometimes blindfolded or tied together by a rope, to punch away at each other until only one was left standing. The audience, mostly white businessmen, would throw coins into the ring to be scooped by the winner. It's unclear how many times Johnson participated in these demeaning events, but even as a youth he knew better money could be made elsewhere.

The key fight of Johnson's early career was a loss to Joe Choynski in 1901. A Polish-Jew with years of fighting experience, Choynski knocked Johnson out in the third round. Making matters worse, Texas Rangers arrested both men after the bout for prizefighting in Texas. The fighters spent nearly two weeks in prison together. To pass the time, Choynski gave Johnson tips on boxing. Choynski encouraged Johnson to feint more, to use his quickness, to be more defensive. By the time the sheriff released them, Johnson had been tutored by one of the best fighters of the day.

Johnson fought all over the country to make his name known, but the best he achieved was recognition as "the colored champion," a position of dubious value. There were a dozen or so excellent Black heavyweights at the time, including Joe Jeannette, Sam McVey, and Sam Langford. Johnson beat them all and then left them to fight among themselves while he pursued the real title.

He was brazen, known to wear pink or purple boxing tights and blow kisses to the shocked men on press row. Though his schooling was limited, he was a grand talker, sometimes affecting a British accent. By the time Johnson scored a two-round knockout of the decrepit 44-year-old former champion Bob Fitzsimmons in 1907, he was a hero to Black sports fans. It was not just for his ring accomplishments but also for the audacious way he carried himself outside the ring. Once, after beating a protégé of John L. Sullivan, Johnson turned to the long-retired legend and said, "How do you like that, Captain John?"

Burns–Johnson boxing fight, Rushcutters Bay, Sydney, December 26,1908, by Charles Kerry.

Johnson's return from Australia sent promoters on a frenzied search to find a white challenger to dethrone the Black champion. McIntosh had shown that a mixed-race bout for the title could be a significant moneymaker, while a portion of the white press began pounding the drums for someone to restore dignity to boxing and the white race. Thus began the era of the "White Hope," a strange time when dozens of strapping young white men left their ranch and factory jobs to enter the seamy world of boxing.

Meanwhile, Johnson stayed busy with other opponents, including the great middleweight champion, Stanley Ketchel. When the two fought in 1909 in Colma, California, there was allegedly an agreement that they would go easy on each other to create a longer fight film. But in the 12th round Ketchel swung hard on Johnson's chin and knocked him down. Angered that their arrangement had been breached, Johnson got up and knocked Ketchel cold. Some of Ketchel's teeth were scattered across the canvas, or embedded in Johnson's right glove.

To the joy of American bigots, former champion Jim Jeffries eventually agreed to come out of retirement and challenge Johnson. Jeffries had spent the past five years enjoying life on his alfalfa farm, but the cry for a white champion along with a massive payday lured him back into training. Jeffries had never been as colorful as Sullivan but was known for his toughness. Wildly strong and seemingly impervious to pain, he'd retired undefeated in 1905. Johnson's detractors had comforted themselves by saying Burns was a fraud, and that Jeffries had been the true champion all along. Jack London, the famous American author, ended one of his articles on Johnson by writing, "Jeff, it's up to you."

Newspaper coverage for Jeffries' return to action was unprecedented. By the time the contest took place in Reno on July 4, 1910, America was ravenous for what promoter Tex Rickard called, "The Battle of the Century." When Johnson received death threats in the mail, the Governor of Nevada sent armed guards to the champion's training camp, just in case someone tried to shoot him.

Johnson was an automobile enthusiast. Ironically, in 1946 he would die in a car crash.

Under the blinding Nevada sun, Johnson casually tormented Jeffries for 14 rounds. Even as men from Jeffries' corner spat racial slurs at him, Johnson fought a calm, relaxed fight. In the 15th round, Johnson sensed the old warhorse was done. With punches as swift and decisive as the blade of a guillotine, he knocked Jeffries to the canvas three times. Members of Jeffries' camp rushed into the ring after the third knockdown, sparing him from more embarrassment. Johnson later described Jeffries as "the gamest man I ever fought."

Johnson also downplayed the race angle.

"My battle with Jeffries was not a contest between a Black man and a white man," he said, "but between two boxers who were out to establish their right to the heavyweight championship of the world, a right I claimed and Jeffries disputed. I beat him and now the matter is settled."

Johnson's win, however, set America into a kind of convulsion. Across the country, vengeful white mobs descended upon Black revelers. In a matter of days there were numerous deaths reported, more than 20 according to some accounts, mostly of Black men, all to do with Johnson's victory in Reno. State authorities ordered theaters to not show the fight film out of fear that more riots and deaths would follow. A drunk St. Louis man armed with a rifle attempted to break into Johnson's Chicago home a few days after the fight. He claimed he had lost his savings by betting on Jeffries. Police believe he would've killed Johnson.

The champion split the press. Many sportswriters appreciated Johnson's skill in the ring. Yet scathing editorials commented on his "uppity" behavior, and how he was inspiring people of his race to act out in similar ways. The *Los Angeles Times* offered Black citizens a chilling warning after the Jeffries bout: "Do not boast too loudly."

Johnson, meanwhile, spent his money lavishly, drove his cars recklessly, and did as he pleased. He was especially bold when it came to his affairs with white women, particularly prostitutes. At a time when mixed marriages were illegal in most states, Johnson pushed his critics to the absolute edge in 1911 when he married a white woman named Etta Duryea, a divorced New York socialite. It was a volatile marriage – Johnson once beat Duryea so badly that she needed hospitalization – and ended with her suicide in 1912. Johnson blamed his wife's death on the pressures of society, though she'd been known for bouts of depression and was often upset by Johnson's infidelities and cruelty. "She was mortally afraid of him," said Duryea's mother.

Though Johnson appeared saddened by Duryea's suicide, he was seen two weeks after the funeral with another white woman, an 18-year-old former prostitute named Lucille Cameron. They'd soon marry, though Cameron's mother claimed Johnson had used "hypnotic powers" to hold Lucille captive. As hysterical as the charges were, an investigation led to Johnson being tried in Chicago on white slavery charges.

By now Johnson's image was at its ebb. Black groups denounced him. A white mob near the courthouse hanged a black-faced dummy, a sign pinned to its chest saying, "THIS IS WHAT WE WILL DO TO JACK JOHNSON." Ultimately, Johnson was brought down by the Mann Act, a confusing law passed in 1910.

Sometimes known as the White Slave Traffic Act, the law prohibited the transporting of women, other than one's wife, across state lines for immoral purposes. Belle Schreiber, a white woman who'd once been Johnson's favorite prostitute, testified against him, telling jurors that he'd brought her from Chicago to Pittsburgh for illicit reasons. Her testimony convinced a jury of white men that Johnson had broken the law, never minding that the trip took place before the Mann Act was passed. In June of 1913, Johnson was fined $1,000 and sentenced to a year and one day in prison.

Rather than accept the penalty, Johnson jumped bail and escaped to Europe. Though he made stage appearances and occasionally stepped into the ring against unheralded opponents, Johnson was soon broke and humiliated.

In 1915, Johnson accepted a bout near Havana, Cuba. The challenger was Jess Willard, a towering rancher from Kansas who had emerged during the White Hope crusade. The slow but mountainous Willard withstood Johnson's attack for 20 rounds before he started battling back. Johnson, 37 and diminished by his time in Europe, faded in the Havana heat. In the 26th round the gigantic Willard connected with an overhand right to Johnson's jaw. The champion collapsed. As the referee counted him out, Johnson rolled over on his back and shielded his eyes from the sun.

Later, Johnson declared he'd agreed to lose the fight in exchange for a lesser prison sentence, a percentage of the fight film earnings, and a chance to come back to America and visit his ailing mother. His claims were nonsense. He merely wanted to discredit Willard, his white conqueror. By 1920, after a lengthy stay in Mexico, Johnson was back in America, serving out his sentence in the U.S. penitentiary in Leavenworth.

Johnson continued boxing after his prison term, but he was no longer relevant. His final official contest was at age 53, though he put on exhibitions well into his 60s. While many of his early bouts are difficult to verify, his record has been given as 77-13-14, with 48 knockouts and 17 no-decisions. His exact statistics may never be known or agreed upon.

Desperate for money, Johnson sold a purported confession to *The Ring* magazine editor, Nat Fleischer,

Johnson defeated Stanley Ketchel by knockout in the 12th round. Colma, California, 1909.

Johnson's reign as champion ended at the hands of Jess Willard. Cuba, 1915.

still claiming his loss to Willard had been prearranged. The story sat in the editor's desk for years. Fleischer eventually published it in the 1950s, but he gave it no credence. After all, film of the bout shows Johnson fighting hard in the early rounds. That wasn't the behavior of a man who had agreed to lose. Still, Fleischer continued to rank Johnson as the greatest heavyweight of all time, rating him over Joe Louis, Jack Dempsey, and Muhammad Ali. As editor of America's premier boxing publication, Fleischer did much to raise awareness of Johnson's career.

Johnson published his memoirs in 1928 and later wrote various newspaper articles and other manuscripts, all swollen with lies and exaggerations. Even if there were kernels of truth to anything he said or wrote, it became impossible to take seriously his plans to rewrite Shakespeare's *Othello*, or his claim of doing undercover work for the U.S. government.

Aside from a triumphant series of personal appearances in Paris in

1932, most of Johnson's later years were spent as a shabby raconteur, spinning his tall tales in various tacky environments. For many years he was featured in Hubert's Museum on New York's 42nd Street. For 10 cents you could meet Johnson and ask him questions. The once mighty champion was now a moth-eaten con man occupying the same grimy space as snake charmers, dog acts, and fortunetellers. The museum's biggest attraction was a flea circus. Johnson once said to columnist John Lardner, "Whatever you write about me, just please remember that I'm a man, and a good one."

In June of 1946, 68-year-old Johnson was killed in a car accident in Raleigh, North Carolina. His death was not treated as major news.

Interest in Johnson was rekindled in the late 1960s thanks to a Broadway play called *The Great White Hope*. Howard Sackler's Pulitzer Prize winning script was based loosely on Johnson's life, with many of the facts blurred. Actor James Earl Jones portrayed the Johnson character, now called "Jack Jefferson," as a rollicking, charismatic rogue. The struggles of this fictionalized Black champion fit the mood of the times, and the play's success led to a film starring Jones. Suddenly Johnson was more significant than he'd been in years, a readymade symbol of a strong Black man fighting white oppression. For a documentary on the fighter, jazz trumpeter Miles Davis recorded a searing album in 1971 called simply, "Jack Johnson." At the height of his fame, Ali often referenced Johnson as "an inspiration."

Authors, filmmakers, and recording artists mined Johnson's story well into the 2000s. In 2018, President Donald Trump pardoned Johnson for his 1913 conviction. "We've righted a wrong," said Trump.

Johnson's legacy is best appreciated from a distance and with careful editing. It is true that he refused to buckle under the racist attitudes of his day, and that he endured excessive and undue harassment. Yet he was also egomaniacal and selfish. He was a brilliant boxer, yet his signature victories were over much smaller

Johnson was a stylish boxer, whose personal life sometimes overshadowed his work in the ring.

"Whatever you write about me, just please remember that I'm a man, and a good one."

– Jack Johnson

men – Burns and Ketchel – and a retired fighter emerging from a long period of inactivity – Jeffries. There is much to admire about Johnson, and much to dislike. But ever since the booming voice of James Earl Jones became attached to him, there began a deliberate rebuilding of the Johnson myth, until it stood like a 20-foot stone statue, and since then, it has been impossible to discuss Johnson without praising him as a heroic figure. Compared with how his lasting image glares before the cult of white shame, whatever else he did hardly matters.

Jack Johnson Statistics	
Heavyweight Champion	1908–1915
Wins	77
KOs	48
Losses	13
Draws	14
No-decisions	19
Total bouts	123

Harry Greb was one of the key figures of 1920s boxing.

3

Harry Greb

Full name:	Edward Henry Greb
Nickname:	The Pittsburgh Windmill
Birthdate:	June 6, 1894; died October 22, 1926
Place of birth:	Pittsburgh, Pennsylvania

Harry Greb died young, but he packed a lot of living in a short time.

He took part in an astonishing 299 bouts, but the legend of Harry Greb rests on two fights.

The first was a 15-round decision over Gene Tunney in New York's Madison Square Garden on May 23, 1922. The victory earned Greb recognition as the American light heavyweight champion. Being the only man to defeat Tunney was a superb accomplishment, but the victory stands out for the way Greb achieved it. It was as close to a complete annihilation as has ever been seen in a boxing ring. Tunney finished the bout on his feet but took such a horrible beating that he probably wished Greb had knocked him out. Then again, knockouts weren't Greb's forte. To fight Greb was like being tortured – death by a thousand cuts.

A journalist from the *Brooklyn Standard Union* summed up the grisly contest in the next day's coverage: "Tunney, smothered by the incessant stream of Greb punches, his face cut into human hamburger, never had a chance after the early exchanges. His nose spurted blood in the first 30 seconds of fighting, his lips were raw and bleeding, his right eye dripped a constant crimson, and his left was barely discernible through the gushing blood."

Left image: Greb (left) squares off with Gene Tunney prior to their first meeting, New York, 1922. Right image: Greb (left) and Tunney prior to their fifth bout, Minnesota, 1925.

The writer chilled readers with the sort of macabre imagery not usually found in the sports pages: "The effect of Tunney's piercing eye, staring out through the blood, was ghastly. It reminded one of a medical diagram, showing the muscles and nerves of the face, utterly devoid of skin."

Tunney had been a marine boxing champion and was unbeaten in 49 professional fights. Yet 15 rounds with Greb left him looking like an animal dragged through a slaughterhouse.

By the time he fought Tunney, Greb had been boxing professionally for nearly a decade and had perfected his frenetic style of fighting. Greb's method was to hit an opponent in the face as many times per minute as his fists could manage. It was, Tunney said, "like fighting an octopus." Indeed, some of Greb's opponents were convinced he'd had a third arm.

Few could endure Greb's merciless drumfire attack. In the years prior to defeating Tunney, he'd fought the best middleweights and light heavyweights of the period, including George Chip, Bob "Caveman" Moha, Mike Gibbons, Tommy Gibbons, Al McCoy, Jack "The Giant Killer" Dillon, Jeff "Ghost" Smith, "Knockout" Brown, Battling Levinsky, Mike McTigue, Bill Brennan, Chuck Wiggins, Billy Miske, Leo Houck, Zulu Kid, Bob Roper, "Gunboat" Smith, and Kid Norfolk. A century later their names may sound like characters from old-time newspaper comics, but they were tough men. Greb fought most of them more than once, and usually got the best of things.

Greb mystified the boxing experts of the day because he never seemed to train. He preferred the trimmings of the American Jazz Age: nightlife, bathtub gin, young women dancing with abandon. Training only got in the way of his carousing. Instead, Greb fought his way into shape. For instance, if he had an important fight scheduled for June, he'd ask his manager to book a few fights for him in April and May, just to stay sharp. This way

Greb mystified the boxing experts of the day because he never seemed to train.

Greb could also get paid, rather than just spend weeks skipping rope in a dull training camp.

Yet Greb's disdain for training was exaggerated. He certainly prepared himself, especially for major bouts. But how could an opponent train for him? How do you prepare to meet a whirling dervish? "He was never in one spot for more than half a second," Tunney recalled.

Determined to solve the riddle of Greb's style, Tunney fought him four more times. Tunney even consulted the lightweight genius, Benny Leonard, for tips. Leonard suggested Tunney concentrate on body shots to slow Greb's momentum. It was a reasonable strategy, but trying to slow Greb was like trying to tame a nest of hornets.

Their second New York bout went to Tunney by 15-round split decision, though fans disputed the verdict, certain that Greb had beaten him again. Tunney also took their third meeting on points, yet Greb hurt Tunney badly in the final round and came very close to winning with his last-minute surge. The fourth Greb–Tunney bout, a 10-round no-decision contest in Cleveland, Ohio, was declared a draw by the newspapers. The fifth Greb–Tunney contest took place in St. Paul, Minnesota, in 1925. It was another close 10-round contest. Newspaper reports gave the edge to Tunney. By then, the two fighters had developed a mutual respect. One year later, Tunney would defeat Jack Dempsey for the heavyweight championship. For the rest of his life, Tunney claimed his fights with Greb had boosted his confidence. "To me he was a great fighter," Tunney said of Greb.

Between the first and fifth bouts with Tunney, Greb fought another collection of top fighters, including Tommy Loughran, Billy Shade, Jimmy Slattery, and Maxie Rosenbloom. Shortly after he'd lost the light heavyweight belt back to Tunney, Greb won the middleweight title by defeating Johnny Wilson in New York.

It was just after his fifth meeting with Tunney that Greb faced the opponent who gave him his second legendary bout. This was Mickey Walker, a fireplug of a fighter known as "The Toy Bulldog." Walker was the welterweight champion. A gutsy little slugger who was one of New York's most popular attractions, Walker stepped up in weight to challenge Greb for the middleweight title. For pure 1920s panache and ribald New York City atmosphere, the pairing of Greb and Walker was unsurpassed.

Accustomed to fighting larger opponents, Greb welcomed a chance to fight a smaller man. However, the betting odds were far in favor of Greb. To make things more interesting, Greb spent the days before the bout putting on an act of public drunkenness. He was seen stumbling around outside of nightclubs looking well-oiled and needing assistance. With his reputation for drinking already in place, the word in New York fight circles was that Greb was taking Walker lightly. The betting odds began shifting. Now Greb could bet on himself and add to his payday.

Top: Harry Greb (right) shakes hands with Mickey Walker after signing the deal to fight for Greb's Middleweight title. New York, 1925.
Bottom: A ticket for the Harry Greb versus Mickey Walker fight.

Greb, wearing oversized training gloves, strikes a pose. Circa 1925.

They fought at the Polo Grounds before 65,000 fans on July 2, 1925. Greb was brilliant as usual, slashing Walker with combinations not taught in any gyms. "He could hit from impossible angles," Walker said. Greb knocked Walker down in one of the early rounds, and nearly knocked him out in the 14th. When it was over, Greb took the 15-round decision by a wide margin. Yet it was what happened, or didn't happen, after the fight that added to his legacy.

There were dozens of differing versions, but the nucleus of the story had the two fighters bumping into each other at a Manhattan speakeasy known as the Silver Slipper. They got into an argument – some accounts say it was over a woman, others say Walker accused Greb of being a dirty fighter – which led to the two drunken pugs fighting in the parking lot. With each retelling of the story, the incident grew more savage. Both men were landing brutal uppercuts, the victim lifted off his feet and flying through the air, crashing onto the hoods of automobiles. It was the sort of mayhem usually seen in Popeye cartoons.

The story was fun but hard to swallow. How could two of the most famous boxers of the 1920s, easily recognized from newspaper coverage, fight in a parking lot of a busy city with no witnesses? Surely, someone would have seen them and rushed to the *Tribune* or the *Daily News* the next morning. Yet there was no mention in the papers of the so-called Silver Slipper slugfest. Still, good stories had a way of spreading, and this was a good one. Of course, there is the old axiom that the better a story is,

He'd had the typical upbringing of a fighter, fending off bullies during his hardscrabble youth in Pittsburgh.

the more likely it's a lie. But that didn't stop this tale from surviving.

Walker kept the story going for years, adding to it and embellishing. In one version he returned to his hotel room and found his girlfriend in bed with Greb. It is possible that Walker nursed the story along because Greb had beaten him so soundly in the ring. With the parking lot rematch, Walker could say he got a bit of revenge. Later in his life, however, when he was living in a Freehold, New Jersey, hospital, Walker received a visit from boxing historian Bert Randolph Sugar. Asked about the infamous street fight with Greb, Walker shrugged. "Nah," he said, "never happened."

What made the story so successful was that it fed into the fantasies of boxing fans, especially those who want to believe that macho men like Greb and Walker can't contain their actions to the ring. In reality, most boxers don't want to fight unless there's money involved. Fighting in a parking lot was for lowlife thugs, not professionals. But the ingredients of the episode – the nightclub milieu, the flow of alcohol, and New York during the Roaring Twenties – fit into Greb's hard-partying playboy persona. If the story wasn't true, it should've been.

Yet there was more to Greb than drinking and chasing women. His life was tragic.

He'd had the typical upbringing of a fighter, fending off bullies during his hardscrabble youth in Pittsburgh. He had his first professional bout at age 19 in 1913 and spent the next several years boxing in the Pittsburgh area.

A 1919 bout with heavyweight Willie Meehan was an indication of Greb's prowess. Awkward with a comic, slapping style, Meehan had been a difficult opponent for the up-and-coming Jack Dempsey. Despite being outweighed by more than 30 pounds, Greb handled Meehan with ease, winning at least nine of 10 rounds at the Duquesne Gardens in Pittsburgh. It was Greb's second time dominating Meehan, which led to speculation that Greb was superior to Dempsey. When Dempsey won the heavyweight championship a few months later, Greb was mentioned as a possible challenger. Yet despite extensive discussion in the sports pages of the time, a Dempsey–Greb battle never took place.

It would've been interesting to see how Dempsey would deal with Greb's whirlwind attack. In 1920, when Greb worked briefly as a sparring partner for Dempsey, witnesses said Greb boxed rings around him. Moreover, Greb had beaten many of the same fighters that Dempsey had fought. It's probable that Dempsey would've been too powerful for Greb, but mythmakers loved touting Greb as the man Dempsey refused to fight. Where Greb was concerned, however, the line between truth and fiction was always a blur.

"More stories are told about Greb than about any man in his field," wrote columnist John Lardner. Perhaps it was Greb's dashing appearance that inspired the myths,

No one knew he had only one working eye and risked permanent blindness each time he fought.

for he was a picturesque character, always immaculately dressed, his hair pomaded down like the male Hollywood stars of the time.

Despite his playboy mystique, Greb was entirely devoted to his wife Mildred, and a doting father to their daughter, Dorothy. Greb's life changed in 1922 when Mildred died of tuberculosis. Friends and family members claimed Greb was never the same without Mildred, and it was only after her death that Greb began enjoying the demimonde.

Greb had another issue – he was losing sight in his right eye. He'd been in the ring with some of the meanest characters in the business, and it was inevitable that Greb would suffer the effects of the constant thumbing and lacing that went on. Greb was also a rule breaker, and many of his bouts came down to hideous displays of fouling. However it happened, Greb spent the later portion of his career half-blind.

An automobile crash shortly after the Walker bout added to Greb's problems. Though he returned to boxing fairly soon, he would tell associates that he wasn't the same fighter after the accident.

Greb's problems were compounded when he became entangled with a married woman named Sally Bronis. A musical theater performer prone to histrionics, she and Greb carried on a secret affair for two years. When he tried to end their relationship, she slit her wrist. Her husband was also suing Greb for turning his wife against him. Last but not least was a rift with his manager, who Greb felt was shortchanging him.

As his physical and financial woes added up, Greb's career was nearing its finish. His reign as middleweight champion ended in 1926 when he lost a close split decision to Tiger Flowers, a Black church deacon from Georgia who was a skilled, if eccentric, boxer. Greb had bested Flowers two years earlier in a no-decision bout, but now it was clear that Greb was slipping. A rematch took place later in the year, but again Flowers won by a split verdict. The largely partisan Greb crowd booed the decision – a pair of Greb's lady friends purportedly attacked the ringside judges after the bout – but in truth their idol had performed badly. He'd fought a desperate, dirty fight, at times trying to throw Flowers out of the ring. *The Herald Statesman* called the contest, "deadly dull . . . a mauling match between a couple of fistic clowns . . ."

In the aftermath of the bout, Greb faced criticism for his dirty tactics, and for the cavalier way he'd treated the middleweight title. No one knew he had only one working eye and risked permanent blindness each time he fought.

He made no official announcement, but Greb was done with fighting. The record he left behind is mind-boggling. His total of 299 ring appearances is among the highest in history (doubly impressive since he crammed them into a 13-year span). It breaks down into a record of 108-8-3, with 49 knockouts and 179 no-decision bouts. Despite his reputation for fouling, he was only disqualified in one bout.

(NEWS photo)

Wham! Harry blocks Tiger and lands mean wallop to face at same time in third

FLOWERS WINS TITLE FROM GREB.—Tiger Flowers, the Georgia deacon, is now middleweight champion of the world. The first colored boxer to hold title, he won decision in fifteen clumsy rounds from Harry Greb at the New Garden. Greb was at his worst during his career as champion. In opinion of majority decision was fair and square. It looked like Greb's fight in thirteenth.—*Story on page 20.*

Greb lost his middleweight title to Tiger Flowers at Madison Square Garden, New York, February 26, 1926.

Within a month of the second loss to Flowers, Greb underwent surgery to remove his right eye and replace it with a prosthetic. Then, in October of 1926, Greb was in another automobile accident that left him with a fractured nose and other injuries. After surgery on his nasal bone in Atlantic City, Greb died in the hospital. He was 32.

According to his brother-in-law, Greb had been despondent in the weeks prior to his death. His "spiritless" mood led his brother-in-law to believe Greb "had a premonition of his fate."

Thousands attended Greb's funeral in Pittsburgh. He was buried next to his wife, Mildred, who had died four years earlier. Among the pallbearers was a handsome, square-jawed man. He wasn't a family member, but the man looked as sad as anyone else at the service. It was Gene Tunney.

Harry Greb Statistics	
Light Heavyweight Champion (USA)	1922–1923
Middleweight Champion	1923–1926
Wins	108
KOs	49
Losses	8
Draws	3
No-decisions	179
No-contests	1
Total bouts	299

Jack Dempsey boosted the popularity of boxing in the 1920s, until it rivaled baseball as America's top sport.

JACK DEMPSEY

Full name:	William Harrison Dempsey
Nickname:	The Manassa Mauler
Birthdate:	June 24, 1895; died May 31, 1983
Place of birth:	Manassa, Colorado

A two-fisted tiger from the west, Jack Dempsey overcame many scandals to become a beloved American figure.

Decades after his reign as heavyweight champion, Jack Dempsey fended off two muggers in Manhattan. The story's details changed with every telling, but it always ended the same way: Dempsey, somewhere past his 70th birthday, flattened both punks and left them lying on the sidewalk.

People loved knowing the old champion could still uncork the left hook. Those creeps got what they deserved for messing with "The Manassa Mauler."

Like John L. Sullivan, Dempsey had a swaggering image. He wasn't a braggart like Sullivan, but he'd roared out of Colorado like a gunfighter. Sunburned and unshaven, with a sneer that told opponents they were in for a bad time, Dempsey was the face of boxing during the 1920s, and arguably the greatest draw in all of sports. His beginnings, however, hardly hinted at the excitement to come.

William Harrison Dempsey was born on June 24, 1895, in Manassa, Colorado, the ninth child of Hyrum and Celia Dempsey. He described himself as "basically Irish, with Cherokee blood from both parents, plus a Jewish strain from my father's great grandmother." Known then

In boxing's first million-dollar gate, Dempsey (right) stopped Georges Carpentier in four rounds. Jersey City, 1921.

as "Harry," his was a childhood of constant travel, ranch life, and, of course, boxing. He and his brothers were so fascinated by tales of great fighters that they turned a chicken coop into a boxing gym and spent their afternoons bashing at a homemade punching bag.

"Out in this little town, Montrose, they used to have fights every day," Dempsey recalled in a 1970 interview. "You'd go to a saloon, fight anybody in the house for 'pass the hat.' Sometimes you got licked, sometimes you'd run like hell, sometimes you'd get a little money."

Dempsey was a teenager when he and his older brother Bernie began working the mining camps of Utah. To earn extra money, they competed in boxing matches against other mineworkers. Dempsey estimated that he'd had 100 or so of these informal fights. Though he was often weakened by hunger or exhausted from minework, he willingly boxed against much older men trying to knock his head off. Dempsey learned how to bob and weave as he came toward an opponent, and how to twist his body to get more force into his punches. "My long-range goal was to become a champion," he wrote, "and now I ate, slept and dreamed of it."

It was Bernie who first took the name "Jack," while young Harry was dubbed "Kid Blackie" because of his jet-black hair. One day Bernie pulled out of a fight and asked Harry to replace him. He also told Harry to take his ring name: Jack

"My long-range goal was to become a champion, and now I ate, slept and dreamed of it."

– Jack Dempsey

Dempsey, borrowed from a popular middleweight of the 1880s.

By 1918, Dempsey had established himself as a compelling young fighter. Fred Fulton, a respected heavyweight who had emerged during the White Hope period, lasted only 18 seconds with him. "Fulton was carried to his corner . . . ," reported the *Dayton Daily News*, "where he was drenched with a bucket of water and even then did not know what happened."

Though his bristly appearance gave him the look of a railroad tramp, Dempsey was actually a polished fighter with a unique style and considerable ring savvy. As he reached his prime, Dempsey was just under 6'2" and weighed approximately 185 pounds. At 24, he was rawboned and vicious; an attacker. The press gave him a slew of colorful, dangerous-sounding nicknames: "The Demon Slugger," "The Man Killer," and finally, "The Manassa Mauler."

Dempsey's long road to stardom led to a scorching hot outdoor ring in Toledo, Ohio, on July 4, 1919. That was where he faced the gigantic heavyweight champion, Jess Willard. Dempsey tore Willard apart, handing him one of the bloodiest defeats in the history of the business. The *San Francisco Bulletin*'s reporter was alarmed to see Willard reduced to "a reeling, battered hulk, dazed, smashed out of all resemblance to anything human."

With a ferocity that thrilled the spectators, Dempsey knocked Willard down seven times in the first round. He continued his terrible assault until Willard's corner stopped the contest after the third. Willard had been an unpopular champion, but Dempsey would usher in America's golden age of sports.

It was Dempsey, his wily manager Jack "Doc" Kearns, and promoter George "Tex" Rickard who helped turn boxing into America's most popular sport alongside baseball. Within months of Dempsey winning the title, professional boxing was legalized in the state of New York – it had been in and out of favor for years, allowed only in certain cities – which led to the establishment of the National Boxing Association (NBA), a sanctioning body that included 13 states.

Though it had grown in popularity since the war, the broader acceptance of boxing was likely due to Dempsey's emergence. It is an old truism that certain fighters somehow reflect the country's ever-changing mood. This was certainly true of Dempsey, who personified the unbridled American energy of the decade. Like never before, the public was looking for icons in sports and entertainment, following the antics of their idols in newspapers and fan magazines, anointing them as mini gods. Like Babe Ruth or Charles Chaplin, Dempsey's every move was newsworthy. But sometimes the news was bad.

In June of 1920 Dempsey found himself in a San Francisco courtroom facing charges of draft evasion. He

Dempsey slamming away at Jess Willard. Toledo, Ohio, 1919.

was eventually cleared of the "slacker" charges, but the highly publicized trial revealed seedy details of Dempsey's past, namely a brief marriage to a Salt Lake City prostitute named Maxine Cates. The trial came at a time when Dempsey stood to make a fortune with personal appearances and movie roles, all of which were now in jeopardy. It also seemed the very business of boxing was at stake, for a heavyweight champion going to prison for cowardice would've destroyed the sport's recent progress. Yet the jury needed only 10 minutes to exonerate Dempsey.

The bout was boxing's first million-dollar gate, pulling in $1,789,238, proof of the Dempsey phenomenon.

The trial cast a shadow over the new champion's image, but the public was still intrigued by him. When Dempsey defended his title against Georges Carpentier of France on July 2, 1921, over 80,000 people crammed into a specially built amphitheater in Jersey City, New Jersey. The bout was boxing's first million-dollar gate, pulling in $1,789,238, proof of the Dempsey phenomenon. It was also the first fight broadcast coast to coast live on the radio, which resulted in an increase in radio sales throughout the country. Adding to the drama was Carpentier's past as a decorated war hero, while Dempsey was still being heckled as a slacker. Yet the cheering that greeted Dempsey showed that his appeal was still strong. Dempsey scored a fourth-round knockout of the Frenchman,

Even in training, Dempsey attracted crowds.

but the event was more notable for its massive audience and the number of dignitaries who had come to see the fighting sensation of the age.

Rickard and Kearns felt Dempsey had to be carefully exhibited to avoid overexposure. After two years of movie roles, stage appearances, trips to Europe, and meaningless exhibitions, Dempsey fought Tommy Gibbons in Shelby, Montana. He won by 15-round decision. Unfortunately, the town went bankrupt after paying the champion.

Two months later, in September of 1923, Dempsey was in New York's Polo Grounds to fight Luis Ángel Firpo of South America. In one of the wildest bouts in boxing annals, the first round saw Dempsey knock Firpo down seven times, while Firpo, whose skills were primitive but brutal, put Dempsey down twice. With both men up and down like alley fighters, the crowd of 85,000 unleashed a tsunami of noise, what writer Paul Gallico called "the greatest sustained mass audience-hysteria ever witnessed in any modern arena." The highlight, however, was near the end of the round when the shaggy Argentine knocked Dempsey flying out of the ring onto the press row. A dazed Dempsey climbed back in – purportedly with help from a few reporters, though this is another story that has been mythicized over the years – and KO'd Firpo at 0:57 of round two. Dempsey retained his title, scored his second million-dollar gate, and showed, once again, that his name was synonymous with thrills.

The fight's hair-raising chaos distracted from the truth about Dempsey. He was getting sloppy. It appeared that Rickard's plan to showcase him infrequently was harmful to Dempsey's ring style. Along with his idleness, the champion had gone Hollywood. Dempsey had already appeared in some movies for Universal Pictures and was soon to be married to actress Estelle Taylor. The feral kid who had spent his youth in brothels and saloons was having the savagery weaned out of him. In August of 1924, Dempsey spent a fortune having his nose remodeled.

While he lived the life of a celebrity, Dempsey's boxing career was unraveling. He split from Kearns over a financial dispute. He was also embroiled in a controversy over not fighting Harry Wills, a top contender who happened to be Black. Rickard had promoted the Johnson–Jeffries bout of 1910 and feared a similar mixed-race fight could enflame the country's racial anxieties. Dempsey always spoke respectfully of Wills but blamed the racial climate of the time for the fight not happening. Fairly or unfairly, Dempsey's failure to fight Wills put a small dent in his reputation.

Meanwhile, Rickard had already selected Dempsey's next opponent. It would be Gene Tunney, an ex-marine with a clever style who had established himself as a leading heavyweight contender.

Dempsey put his title on the line against Tunney on September 23, 1926, at Philadelphia's new open-air Sesquicentennial Stadium. It was another of Rickard's masterpieces of promotion, drawing an astounding 120,757 to the venue. But three years had passed since the Firpo fight, and Dempsey's Hollywood lifestyle had only softened him. Rain poured down throughout the contest, and the sight of Dempsey shambling forward in the wet ring, his face streaming with blood, was heartbreaking. Tunney won easily by 10-round decision. What stuck with the public, however, was Dempsey's grace in defeat. By the final bell his eyes were so swollen that he could barely see. "Take me to him," he said. His handlers guided Dempsey across the ring so he could congratulate Tunney, his conqueror.

Later, when Estelle saw his ruined face, Dempsey shrugged.

"Honey," he said, "I forgot to duck."

In an example of America's fickle nature, losing the title made Dempsey more popular than ever.

The following June saw him fight Jack Sharkey at Yankee Stadium. It was another million-dollar gate, proving Dempsey had retained his allure. Though he looked rusty and slow, the end of the fight was vintage Dempsey. In the seventh round Sharkey turned to the referee to complain that Dempsey had fouled him. Right then, Dempsey landed a left hook to Sharkey's face. Sharkey collapsed and was counted out. When a reporter asked Dempsey if it was fair to hit Sharkey when he wasn't looking, Dempsey scoffed. "What was I supposed to do?" he said. "Write him a letter?"

Next for Dempsey was a rematch with Tunney, which would result in one of the most discussed fights of the century.

On September 22, 1927, 104,943 spectators filled the recently built Soldier Field stadium in Chicago, curious to see if Dempsey could regain the title.

For the first six rounds it was a repeat of their first fight, with Dempsey in futile pursuit of Tunney. Then, in the seventh, Dempsey knocked Tunney into the ropes and then fired a fusillade of punches, all connecting squarely on Tunney's face and chin. The crowd erupted. This was what they'd paid to see.

Tunney fell backwards, sinking into the canvas like a warship that had been blasted in half. He sat there with a dreamy look on his face, looking up at the referee, realizing at last what it felt like to receive the full Dempsey attack. The massive throng in Chicago and the millions more listening to the radio broadcast couldn't believe what was happening. Dempsey was on the verge of reclaiming the championship.

Dempsey and his promoter, George "Tex" Rickard. The pair turned boxing into a million-dollar sport.

Dempsey hovers over Luis Firpo in their memorable battle at the Polo Grounds. New York, 1923.

The hitch was in a recent rule that demanded a fighter scoring a knockdown wait in the furthest neutral corner while the referee counted. Dempsey's camp had asked for this rule to be enforced in Chicago, but Dempsey seemed oblivious to such niceties. He hovered over Tunney, panting and wild-eyed.

"I was the jungle fighter," Dempsey wrote years later, "so completely set in my ways I couldn't accept new conditions. I was used to standing over my opponents to make sure that when I pounded them down, they stayed down."

As precious seconds ticked by, referee Dave Barry struggled to move Dempsey to a neutral corner. He finally began his count over the dazed champion, though it was estimated that approximately 14 seconds passed before Tunney rose. Tunney survived to the bell and went on to win the fight by 10-round decision, but he would hear for the rest of his life that Dempsey was denied the championship on a technicality.

The fight's gate receipts totaled $2,658,660, a record for a live sporting event that stood untouched for decades. Adjusted for inflation, the gate for Dempsey–Tunney II would be approximately $47 million in today's dollars, still among the top earning fights of all time. As controversy brewed over the Chicago "long count," Rickard proposed a third Tunney bout. Dempsey declined, quitting the business at 32.

Dempsey was serious about retiring, but the 1929 Wall Street crash and a series of failed business ventures left him broke. He resumed boxing.

From August of 1931 to September of 1932, Dempsey put on exhibitions throughout the American heartland and Canada, entertaining people who couldn't have traveled to see him in New York, Chicago, or Philadelphia. It was unglamorous, with stories of Dempsey in some dismal, backwater arena, sitting between rounds on an upside-down milk crate. Still, the tour put some money in his pocket and took his mind off his pending divorce from Estelle. Like many others during the Great Depression, Dempsey was just another fellow trying to get by. He described it as "somewhat humiliating," but the yearlong exhibition tour endeared him to the public all over again.

During the war years he joined the Coast Guard at age 47. Dempsey relished his role as a patriotic elder statesman. However, where Dempsey truly flourished was as a restaurant owner.

Established in 1935 on New York's Eighth Avenue, "Jack Dempsey's Restaurant" became a city staple. When it moved to Broadway and 49th Street, it was bigger still. Dempsey was there most nights, seated at his favorite table, calling everybody "pal." Generations of people would boast that they'd seen the great Jack Dempsey in the restaurant window, as big as life. He'd become a New York icon, on par with the Statue of Liberty and the Empire State Building.

Chaos during the infamous "long count" fight. Gene Tunney is down, while referee Dave Barry ushers Dempsey to a neutral corner. Chicago, 1927.

But even as Dempsey enjoyed a satisfying retirement there was a dangerous blow to his image. In 1964 *Sports Illustrated* ran a scandalous article by Kearns alleging Dempsey had fought Willard with plaster in his gloves. Dempsey sued the magazine for libel and was vindicated out of court, but the story inspired unfortunate talk about Dempsey's "loaded" gloves. It was an ugly falsehood from Kearns, who had downgraded Dempsey since they'd parted ways 40 years earlier. The glove story was just another storm for Dempsey to endure, as was the end of his restaurant, shuttered in 1975 when new owners broke his lease. Closing his cherished business, Dempsey wrote, "damn near killed me."

Dempsey's boxing record is now given as 61-6-8, with 50 knockouts and six no-decision bouts, though many of his early fights were not recognized as official contests, and not even Dempsey could've provided the exact time and place when his career began. Regardless, mere statistics can't reflect his impact on the sport, or his place in the culture. He was an American original, and remained so until his death in 1983, just a few weeks before his 88th birthday.

In a 1959 memoir, Dempsey wrote that he never quite understood why the public embraced him after he'd lost to Tunney. The American people, he wrote, "have been wonderfully kind to me. Far kinder than any man deserves." He added that being the heavyweight champion was a wonderful experience. "I was lucky – the right guy at the right time."

Dempsey knew what he meant to the public. That's probably why he told the story about the muggers. He told it more than once, always saying it happened just a few weeks ago. He knew people loved it. Was it true? Who knows? But it served a purpose. His last official bout had been against Tunney in Chicago. But in this story, there'd be no long count. The muggers stayed down. Dempsey's legend stood tall.

Jack Dempsey Statistics	
Heavyweight Champion	1919–1926
Wins	61
KOs	50
Losses	6
Draws	8
No-decisions	6
Total bouts	81

Benny Leonard was an idol for Jewish fans in New York and across the country.

5

Benny Leonard

Full name:	Benjamin Leiner
Nickname:	The Ghetto Wizard
Birthdate:	April 7, 1896; died April 18, 1947
Place of birth:	New York, New York

He began as a hero to Jewish fans and ended as a champion for all times.

Boxing is a skill, not an art. Yet anyone who saw Benny Leonard in the ring felt they were watching an artist at work.

Always on his toes, bouncing, jabbing, dodging, he was the consummate ring tactician. He used his left jab like a fencing master using a foil, while his right hand was like a street fighter's weapon, as potent as a sock filled with lead bearings. And if you happened to hit Leonard and hurt him, he'd be so clever about it that you wouldn't even know you'd connected. He was a genius at trickery, at hitting and not getting hit. If he wasn't an artist, he was damned close.

From May 1917 to the time of his first retirement in 1925, Leonard lorded over the 135-pound class for seven years, seven months, and 18 days, longer than any other lightweight champion. When boxing historian Nat Fleischer wrote Leonard's biography in the 1940s and called it *Leonard the Magnificent*, no one accused Fleischer of hyperbole. He was simply echoing what many felt, especially the Jewish fans who had always hailed Leonard as their Superman. In a period when many Jewish boxers won championships and drew crowds, Leonard reigned supreme over a talented lot.

Three great ones: Johnny Dundee (left), Beau Jack (center) and Leonard, during his military service, circa 1942.

He was born Benjamin Leiner in Manhattan on April 7, 1896. Raised in the Lower East Side's Jewish Ghetto, he had to fight to protect himself. It was a rough neighborhood marked by poverty and overcrowding. Friction between new arrivals and older immigrants was ongoing, while newspapers reported on malnourished children fainting in schoolrooms. Crimes ranged from petty robberies and landlord scams to spectacular murders; violent gangs from other parts of the city often dumped their dead victims in the area.

Despite his mother's disapproval, Benny took up boxing. Different sources say his name was changed either because a ring announcer mispronounced it as "Leonard," or he needed an alias to keep his mother from knowing he'd taken up the distasteful pastime of fighting for money. Yet his mother was also partly responsible for Leonard developing his great defensive technique; if he came home with his face unmarked, she'd never know how her son spent his spare time.

Leonard had his first professional bout at age 15. He lost. In fact, he lost four times during his first year of competition. Most young fighters would've been discouraged, but Leonard was diligent. He improved each year. His brothers Charlie and Joey were also in the boxing game, but Benny surpassed them. At 19, he attracted serious attention by knocking out veteran Joe Mandot in Harlem. With this performance, *The Buffalo News* called Leonard "a first-class championship prospect."

Leonard had a patrician's air about him. His slick black hair would be combed by a handler between rounds to make Leonard look refreshed, even in a tough fight. Realizing his appearance was part of his allure, Leonard developed a post-fight signature of smoothing his hair back with his hands, a signal to his Jewish fans that he'd won easily and hadn't even mussed his hair. His admirers would go bonkers at the gesture. Their Benny was untouchable.

Fighting at a time when professional boxing was still illegal in many states, Leonard took part in 121 no-decision bouts, contests where no winner was declared unless there was a knockout. These bouts were designed to curb gambling, and give boxing more of an elite, sportsman's feel, rather than the rough, unruly atmosphere of mere "prizefighting." A boxer such as Leonard could earn money by taking as many of these no-decision affairs as his schedule would allow. It was a chance for him to bring his unique skills to various locations and let his legend grow. The customers would pay just to watch Leonard's footwork, while his opponents seemed utterly baffled by his agility and speed.

Leonard's skill bemused his trainers. Frail and small-boned, he was one of the least likely physical specimens to take up fighting. True, he lived a clean life and was dedicated to his profession, but even those closest to him were mystified as to how such a delicate young man could be so dominating. "His main asset was his ability to think," said Hall of Fame trainer Ray Arcel. "He had the sharpest mind."

He also had a sharp punch, which he apparently saved for special occasions.

Aside from his 121 no-decision bouts, he posted a sterling 89-6-1 record with 70 knockouts. When there was something more at stake than amusing the ringsiders and collecting a quick payday, Leonard could knock opponents into stupors. The newspapers liked to describe him as a nice Jewish boy, but the mild-mannered champion who wore the Star of David on his trunks could provide thrills on par with anyone.

The night in May 1917 when he lifted the lightweight title from Freddie Welsh in Manhattan was just such an occasion. Leonard stopped Welsh at 1:15 of the ninth round, knocking him down three times before referee Kid McPartland stopped the contest and raised Leonard's hand. Welsh was a British fighter, and an unpopular one at that. As the *Brooklyn Daily Eagle* reported, "when the crowd realized a New Yorker had won the world's championship, bedlam broke loose. The rush to the ringside broke down the railings, chairs and press box, and the special police were powerless to check the avalanche of human beings tearing toward the ring."

The importance of Leonard's victory was summed up by one *Eagle* headline. In large print it boomed that the 21-year-old, "BRINGS LIGHTWEIGHT TITLE TO AMERICA!" Considering that heavyweight champion Jess Willard was inactive, and that the First World War was draining the boxing landscape, a Jewish-American lightweight champion from New York

Jack Dempsey the animalistic street fighter (left) poses with Leonard, the classy ring technician.

Leonard's title reign included eight successful defenses and numerous non-title bouts, but it was the opposition that made it legendary.

was an uplifting story, just the thing to keep the business humming stateside.

Leonard's title reign included eight successful defenses and numerous non-title bouts, but it was the opposition that made it legendary. Leonard's opponents included Johnny Kilbane, Ted "Kid" Lewis, Johnny Dundee, Willie Ritchie, Charlie White, Rocky Kansas, and Lew Tendler, most of whom would one day be enshrined in the International Boxing Hall of Fame. Leonard fought most of them more than once, and if a bout was close, he usually won convincingly in a rematch.

Many would say Leonard's most memorable fight was against Richie Mitchell at Madison Square Garden in 1921. He'd knocked Mitchell out in seven rounds a few years earlier and figured this rematch would have a similar outcome. But after a conversation with the notorious gambler, Arnold Rothstein, Leonard had vowed to knock Mitchell out in one round. Intrigued, Rothstein said he would bet $25,000 on Leonard scoring a first-round knockout. "He said he would give me a piece of the bet for nothing," Leonard said. "Well, Arnie was a good friend and I didn't want to disappoint him. I also wanted to pick up some of that money, so I tore into Mitchell at the opening bell."

It appeared Leonard would make good on his promise to Rothstein. He battered Mitchell to the canvas three times in the first two minutes. Yet as the round neared its end, Mitchell landed a right to the chin that knocked Leonard down and nearly out. It was a dizzy Leonard who rose at a count of nine, barely able to stand. "I was in worse shape than Mitchell had been in," he said.

As close to losing his championship as any titleholder had ever been, Leonard boxed carefully for a few rounds. When he had fully regained his senses, Leonard finally stopped

Mitchell at 1:55 of the sixth. The ending was brutal, with Leonard knocking Mitchell down another three times and then, as *The Buffalo News* put it, came "the dreadful scene of a helpless man being pummeled into unconsciousness."

The fight was an immediate sensation. The *Daily News* called it, "one of the most furious bouts ever seen in the prize ring." Fifty years later, sportswriters who had witnessed it still referred to Leonard–Mitchell II as the best fight they'd ever seen. The punch line, of course, was that Rothstein hadn't placed his bet. He'd purportedly fixed the 1919 World Series, and had helped organize the American Mafia, but on this night he couldn't find any takers.

Mitchell figured in another Leonard bout in 1923, though it was his brother, "Pinky," who fought Leonard that night at the Dexter Park Pavilion in Chicago. When Leonard knocked out Pinky in the 10th, Richie believed his brother had been fouled. He jumped into the ring and started taking swings at referee Davey Miller. This resulted in such a riot that several people at ringside were injured, including invited city officials who ended up with bloody noses. The contest had been presented as a society fundraiser, but the well-heeled ladies in attendance were shocked by the melee. A United Press headline roared: "WOMEN SCREAM AS GORE SPILLS."

The Mayor of Chicago made a motion to ban the sport in the city, but by 1923 boxing was too ingrained in the public consciousness to be outlawed. The rise in popularity was mostly because of Jack Dempsey, but also thanks to Leonard, who was regarded as a snazzier flipside to the fierce heavyweight champion.

Another of Leonard's interesting opponents was Jack Britton, a fighter who was nearly Leonard's equal in terms of ring talent, and one of the few who kept a busier schedule, finishing his career with a reported 345 bouts. Britton and Leonard had met twice previously in no-decision affairs, with most reporters giving the nods to Leonard. But with Britton claiming the welterweight title in 1919, it seemed logical that

Leonard would one day come up to the heavier class and challenge for the laurels at 147 pounds. They fought for Britton's title on June 6, 1922, at the Bronx Velodrome. In the 13th round Leonard hit Britton with a body punch that dropped the welterweight champion to his knees. Then the unexpected happened.

Britton, still down, was complaining to referee Patsy Healey that he'd been fouled. But as Britton pleaded his case, Leonard rushed forward and, inexplicably, struck Britton while he was still kneeling. Healey immediately disqualified Leonard. Many on press row wondered if they'd just witnessed a sham.

Twenty-six years later, Leonard's trainer, Mannie Seamon, told the *Sunday Empire News* that the bout had indeed been prearranged for Leonard to lose. According to Seamon, Leonard's manager, Billy Gibson, worked out an agreement with Britton's manager, "Dumb" Dan Morgan. The shame of the story, if true, is that Britton was past his best and Leonard probably could've beaten him on this night, becoming one of the first fighters to win titles in two weight classes, and the first lightweight champion to win the welterweight title.

Though Seamon's story is questionable, Leonard wasn't above a bit of prearranged deception. According to Arcel, Leonard often agreed to treat his opponents gently. This was the only way to get people in the ring with him. Seamon also admitted that Leonard occasionally carried an opponent, doing just enough to win but making the other man look good enough that a more lucrative rematch could be scheduled for the near future. This wasn't unusual in the era, and other fighters of superior skill have been accused of doing the same. Moreover, Leonard was certainly capable of such a thing. After all, this was a man who would sometimes spar with two fighters at the same time, keeping both at bay with his rapid left hand.

The odd result of the Britton bout notwithstanding, Leonard remained important to Jewish fans. Budd Schulberg, who as a boy kept a scrapbook of Leonard's exploits,

Leonard (left) and Dempsey, horsing around for some servicemen.

summed up the significance of Leonard in the foreword to a 1997 book called *When Boxing Was a Jewish Sport.* With great emotion, Schulberg recalled how Leonard's success, "sent a message to Jewish ghettos across America: You may think of us as pushcart peddlers and money grubbers. But we can climb into the ring with you, the best you have to offer, and maybe you can knock us down (as Richie Mitchell knocked down the Great Benny) but you can't keep us down. We've got the skills and the courage to beat you at your own game. Ready or not, we're moving up!"

As had happened with Dempsey, Leonard found his way to Hollywood. He starred in a handful of cheaply made melodramas with Leonard usually playing a version of himself, a feisty little guy who could fight. He also had some minor success in vaudeville as a dancer and actor. It seemed he was preparing himself for life after boxing, a topic that was already on his mind. By 1925, struggling to make the 135-pound limit and

He fought often, and his name still had commercial appeal, but his once marvelous reflexes were gone.

having already earned a fortune, he retired as lightweight champion. That should've been the perfect end to a brilliant career, but Leonard couldn't stay out of the ring.

Seven years after Leonard's retirement he mounted a sorry comeback. By now he was 35, balding, and broke after the 1929 stock market crash. He fought often, and his name still had commercial appeal, but his once marvelous reflexes were gone. "He was washed up," Arcel recalled. "But he was dead broke."

The comeback ended in October of 1932. In Madison Square Garden, where he'd scored so many beautiful victories, Leonard faced a young firecracker named Jimmy McLarnin. Leonard boxed well in the fight's opening minutes, but McLarnin knocked him down in the second round and took over the fight.

Referee Art Donovan consulted with Leonard's corner after each round, telling Arcel, "Don't let him get hurt." With Leonard unable to defend himself, Donovan finally stopped the contest at 2:55 of the sixth. Leonard took it well. "He shook his head," reported the *Brooklyn Daily Eagle*, "smiled wanly at some ringside friends and then wandered to his corner."

Later, Leonard joked with reporters in his dressing room. He said it was good to lose once in a while. Of his six career losses, the first four had taken place when he was a 15-year-old novice, and the sixth was at the end of his career at 36. In between there was only the sketchy disqualification loss to Britton. Indeed, losing was rare for Leonard.

Still needing money, Leonard reinvented himself as a referee. With the same work ethic he'd possessed as a fighter, Leonard officiated more than 120 bouts over the next 16 years. During World War II he joined the Merchant Marine and served as a boxing instructor at

Hoffman Island in Lower New York Bay. When the war ended Leonard resumed his work as an official.

In April of 1947, while refereeing a contest at New York's St. Nicholas Arena, 51-year-old Leonard collapsed. Attendants carried him to the dressing room where he was pronounced dead. He'd had a heart attack. The program continued in the arena; the crowd was unaware that one of the world's great fighters had passed away. It was a bleak end for Leonard, his dead body lying in the dank catacombs of a small, dingy arena on West 66th Street.

Tributes poured in from sportswriters for several days. Leonard was no longer just a Jewish icon. He was now remembered as one of the greatest lightweights who ever lived, a distinction he still held a century after his heyday. It was a remarkable legacy for a boy who tried to keep his boxing career a secret from his mother.

Benny Leonard Statistics	
Lightweight Champion	1917–1925
Wins	89
KOs	70
Losses	6
Draws	1
No-decisions	121
No-contests	3
Total bouts	220

Boxing's perpetual motion man, Henry Armstrong, was the only fighter to own championships in three weight classes simultaneously.

Henry Armstrong

Full name:	Henry Melody Jackson Jr.
Nickname:	Homicide Hank, Hurricane Henry
Birthdate:	December 12, 1912; died October 22, 1988
Place of birth:	Columbus, Mississippi

A publicity stunt conceived by his manager put "Homicide Hank" on the road to everlasting fame.

This story begins with a single page from a newspaper floating in the wind.

It twisted in the air down the streets of St. Louis, as if to some predetermined destination. A young man was walking home from his job at the Missouri-Pacific Railroad when he saw the page flying toward him. "It just fell on the ground in front of me," he recalled many years later, "and the wind just stopped."

He picked up the loose page and noticed an article about the colorful Cuban boxer, Kid Chocolate, and the impressive payday he'd earned for a recent fight. With visions of fame and a new Cadillac in his head, Henry Jackson Jr. decided at that moment to become a fighter. Boxing fans would know him as Henry Armstrong.

He told the story of the news page differently over the years, but always presented it as if his entry into boxing was through a kind of divine guidance. It's more likely that he was inspired to fight by his coworkers at the railroad, many of whom were part-time boxers and had noted his compact physique and high energy. However it happened, Armstrong would leave his mark on the history of boxing.

He had the hard luck background common among

A familiar sight from the 1930s – Armstrong tearing into an opponent.

fighters. He was born on December 12, 1912, in Columbus, Mississippi. He was the 11th of 15 children born to parents descended from slaves and plantation owners. When boll weevils destroyed the cotton fields where his father worked, the Jackson family moved on to St. Louis. Henry's family was so poor that he took any work he found, which was how he ended up driving railroad spikes with a sledgehammer. And then along came a sheet from a newspaper, nudging him down a new career path.

He picked up fights wherever he could, learning to box along the way. Seeking success out west, Henry and a friend hopped rail cars and spent 11 days journeying across America's "hobo jungles." When they reached Los Angeles, Henry took his friend's name: Armstrong.

Alternating between the amateurs and the pros, Armstrong failed to make the 1932 U.S. Olympic team and lost four of his first five professional bouts. This might've dampened the enthusiasm of other young men but not Armstrong. By 1935 he was recognized as the featherweight champion of California, or the "western" champion.

He'd developed a hyper-aggressive style of fighting. It was an unforgettable image, the smallish Armstrong standing with his legs spread wide, crouching, his arms crossed over his face, stalking forward. With his fists pumping like pistons, he'd pin a rival on the ropes and hammer at him, then fire his right hand upwards like springing a catapult. The press dubbed his chugging, nonstop attack as "the perpetual motion." Armstrong's victims included some reputable fighters: Rodolfo Casanova, Midget Wolgast, Baby Arizmendi, Juan Zurita, Mike Belloise, Frankie Klick, and Benny Bass.

Armstrong's relentless style was matched by his relentless schedule. He fought constantly, often two or three times per month. In 1937, Armstrong won 27 fights, 26 by knockout. By age 27 he'd had nearly 100 professional bouts.

And by then he'd attracted the trio of men who would shape his future.

Al Jolson, the famous entertainer, wanted to buy Armstrong's contract. As Armstrong told it, Jolson's wife, Ruby Keeler, knew a gangster named Eddie Mead who had once helped her out by paying for dance lessons. To pay Mead back, she suggested that Jolson buy the fighter's contract and bring in Mead to manage him. Mead, in turn, recruited George Raft, a popular actor known for his underworld connections. Raft helped pay off Armstrong's old manager, a Kentucky gambler named Wirt Ross.

With Jolson, Raft, and Mead installed as Armstrong's new brain trust, the next step was to make him famous. The concern was that Armstrong would remain secondary to the heavyweight champion, Joe Louis, who'd taken the country by storm. "So they came up with the idea that I had to get super popular, colossal," Armstrong said. "They had those words in Hollywood – colossal, stupendous, and all like that."

It was decided that Armstrong needed a gimmick that would set him apart from other fighters. Mead proposed that Armstrong aim for not one championship but would win three at the same time – featherweight, lightweight, and welterweight.

A few fighters had won titles in two or three weight classes in the past, but no one had ever claimed three at once. Such a feat was inconceivable.

Without the junior or half-step weight classes that would proliferate the sport in years to come, this stunt would require Armstrong to fight at 126, 135, and then 147 pounds in a short time span. (Additionally, there was one champion per weight class in 1937, rather than multiple titlists as in the contemporary era, meaning Armstrong would have to meet the best man at each weight, rather than chase the easiest of the pack.) It was a leap in logistics that staggered the imagination. But as you might expect from a man who fought three times per month and shot through opponents like a torpedo, Armstrong liked the idea.

The mission began on October 29, 1937, at Madison Square Garden in New York. Using his high-pressure style, Armstrong stopped featherweight champion Petey Sarron at 2:37 of the sixth round. But with one title down and two to go, there was a problem.

Armstrong had wanted to tackle the three weight classes in ascending order, but lightweight champion Lou Ambers declared he wouldn't fight Armstrong right away. Instead, Armstrong was forced to leapfrog over the lightweight class to challenge welterweight champion Barney Ross. Armstrong was accustomed to fighting men in the featherweight range, but now he was facing a full-blown welterweight. Even though Ross agreed to come in at 142 pounds instead of the standard limit of 147, he'd still be heavier than most of Armstrong's past opponents. Moreover, Ross was a highly regarded champion.

After several weeks of drinking beer and eating potatoes, Armstrong weighed in for his welterweight title fight. He was somewhere south of 140, but he'd made the division's minimum. When the fight was postponed for several days because of foul weather, he started losing weight, while Ross rehydrated. Who knows what either man weighed when they finally did battle at the Madison Square Garden Bowl in Long Island on May 31, 1938. Armstrong later reckoned he was spotting Ross approximately 25 pounds. Regardless, with a second

Henry Armstrong (center) fights Jimmy Garrison in a successful defense of his World Welterweight championship in Los Angeles, California. October 24, 1939.

title in reach, Armstrong put on the performance of his career.

Ross fought well in the early rounds but gradually succumbed to Armstrong's ceaseless, suffocating attack. After the 12th, it seemed the champion's corner might concede. However, the exhausted Ross refused to quit in front of nearly 30,000 spectators.

"He was out on his feet," Armstrong said in 1955, "but he

Armstrong in training for a bout.

wouldn't give up. I knew I was way ahead on points, so I eased up during the final rounds, although I tried to make it look good."

Armstrong often claimed he carried Ross in the late rounds, but like the story about the floating newspaper page, Armstrong never described the Ross fight the same way twice. On one occasion he said his manager received a signal from Ross's corner and then ordered him to let Ross survive to the last bell. Yet another time Armstrong said he made the decision on his own, and that he'd even discussed it with Ross in mid-ring during a clinch.

Though it is part of boxing folklore, Armstrong's description of events is questionable. Most newspaper reports of the fight depict him battering Ross during the final rounds. The Buffalo *Courier Express* described Armstrong landing a left hook in the 14th "that spun Ross half around and sent a bloody spray across the ring." It doesn't sound like Armstrong was showing Ross mercy.

Nevertheless, Armstrong won a 15-round decision and left New

Fearing the ref might deny him his third belt, Armstrong spent the later rounds swallowing his own blood rather than spitting it out.

York with the welterweight title in his possession.

Three months later, in August of 1938, Armstrong and Ambers met at Madison Square Garden for the lightweight crown. It was a brutal contest with Armstrong scoring two knockdowns early, while Ambers' punches tore a gash over Armstrong's left eye and gave him a terrible cut inside his mouth. As the referee took note of Armstrong constantly spitting blood all over the ring, he warned the challenger that the fight might be stopped. Fearing the ref might deny him his third belt, Armstrong spent the later rounds swallowing his own blood rather than spitting it out.

Both fighters banged away at each other in the final minutes of the bout, neither able to land a deciding punch. When the action ceased, Armstrong was awarded a 15-round split decision. Although some in attendance felt Ambers had deserved a draw and jeered the scorecards, most felt Armstrong had earned the win. The *Brooklyn Daily Eagle* hailed it as "one of the greatest championship battles of any class ever fought in the Garden or any other ring."

Armstrong's nine-month campaign to win three titles simultaneously had reached a successful conclusion. But later that night, as a doctor tended his wounds, Armstrong felt empty. He was boxing's first triple champion, but something was missing. He didn't feel colossal. The crowd had booed him. He also wasn't sure that winning three titles meant much. He wondered, "Where do I go from here?"

Many thought Armstrong was showing signs of burnout. Mead was still pushing him to fight frequently. He fought 12 times in 1939, and even found time to star in a low budget, independent movie based loosely on his life. It was a clunker called *Keep Punching*, which was financed partly with Armstrong's money. "When you're champ," he wrote in his memoir, "you have to keep going to stay on top. You have only a few years in which to make your money, and after that you're just another has-been."

Becoming the triple champion earned Armstrong some accolades, and he shared a few magazine covers with Louis, but it didn't make him into an overnight star. Instead, the amazing feat drew accusations that he and his managers were monopolizing the weight classes. By December of 1939, the National Boxing Association and the New York State Athletic Commission ruled that a boxer could not be champion in more than one weight class at a time. As a result of the ruling, Armstrong would be history's sole triple titlist. No one else would get the chance.

Armstrong relinquished the featherweight title because he could no longer get down to 126 pounds. Then, one year after winning the lightweight title from Ambers, he lost it back to Ambers on a 15-round decision. This left Armstrong with only the welterweight title, which he defended a record 19 times.

In October of 1940, however, Armstrong lost his remaining title to Fritzie Zivic. In losing a 15-round decision, Armstrong took so much punishment that he could barely see in the late rounds. "The picture of this blind, bleeding gladiator groping, yet punching, ranks with the great fistic scenes of all time," wrote the *Brooklyn Daily Eagle*. In the final seconds of the last round, Armstrong fell from fatigue at the bell. It seemed the perpetual motion man had finally run out of steam.

On January 17, 1941, more than 23,000 fans crammed into the Garden to see if Armstrong could regain the title from Zivic, a gathering believed to be the largest Garden crowd to that time. What they saw was Zivic butcher Armstrong again, cutting him badly over the eyes, until referee Art Donovan ended the contest at 0:52 of the 12th round. Believing they'd seen him for the last time, the crowd thundered in appreciation for the defeated Armstrong as he left the ring.

Armstrong lived the high life in retirement, but he grew restless. He returned to boxing in the summer of 1942, 18 months after losing to Zivic.

This final act of Armstrong's career was lucrative. The old combination of Meade, Jolson, and Raft had dissolved. Mead had dropped dead on a city street in 1942, so Armstrong sought a new manager, George Moore. Armstrong never spoke ill of Mead but would claim this latter part of his career was more profitable for him than his days as a triple champion.

Armstrong won another 40 bouts, with a few losses and draws mixed in. He even got some revenge against Zivic, earning a 10-round decision over him in San Francisco, though by then the bout meant little. Zivic had already lost the welterweight title to Freddie Cochrane and was struggling through his own comeback.

Though he still had some firepower, Armstrong faltered against the younger fighters of the day. In 1943 he dropped a 10-rounder to Beau Jack, a force of nature from Georgia who was nearly a replica of a prime Armstrong. Later in the year Armstrong lost on points to Sugar

In May of 1939, Armstrong defended his welterweight title in London's Haringay Arena, defeating Britain's Ernie Roderick by 15-round decision.

Ray Robinson, a young welterweight star who considered Armstrong one of his idols. "It was a disgusting

There were marriages, divorces, and bad investments. Armstrong ended up penniless.

fight," Armstrong said, angry that Robinson had spent the entire contest on the move. "I couldn't get him."

Armstrong's final bout was in February of 1945, a 10-round loss to Chester Slider in Oakland. He knew he was finished. Armstrong's official record is believed to be 152-22-10, with 100 knockouts, though historians dicker over the exact numbers.

He traveled the world that year, putting on exhibitions for the troops overseas. Then, while visiting Egypt, Armstrong experienced a religious awakening. This led to him becoming an ordained minister, which played a major part in the remainder of his life.

There were marriages, divorces, and bad investments. Armstrong ended up penniless, suffering from dementia and a myriad of health problems. He died in 1988 at age 75.

Much of what we know about Armstrong comes from his 1956 memoir, *Glory, Gloves, and God: An Autobiography*. In it he described his problems with alcohol and the pitfalls of fame. A fascinating part of the book was his description of a long-forgotten 1940 bout with Ceferino Garcia, a hard-punching Filipino fighter who was the middleweight champion.

Armstrong had beaten Garcia in the past and was challenging him for the middleweight crown. At Gilmore Stadium in Los Angeles, Armstrong punished Garcia for 10 rounds. To the ringsiders it appeared he'd done enough to win. Strangely, the verdict was a draw. Armstrong revealed in his book that he'd refused a payoff to throw the contest. This, he believed, resulted in the fight's outcome being affected by gamblers. "Let it be said here, for the record, that Garcia had nothing whatever to do with this bribe," Armstrong wrote. "His hands were clean."

Armstrong varied the story over the years, the money offered being $15,000 in one telling, $75,000 in another.

The press had been suspicious of the bout before a punch was thrown. Garcia had a major fight with Ken Overlin scheduled a month later in New York, and it wouldn't be good business for him to lose his title. Some of the more experienced journalists were predicting the bout would be called a draw no matter what happened. They must've loved the result. And they must've laughed when the state commissioner defended the draw by saying referee George Blake, solely responsible for the verdict, had penalized Armstrong for fouls. Blake, incidentally, never refereed another fight.

Armstrong and his admirers often pointed to this bout as the tragedy of his career. A win would've made Armstrong a champion in four weight classes, which would've been another history-making first.

Did gamblers get to the referee to make sure Armstrong didn't win? It's possible. "If I win," Armstrong said years later, "his life wasn't worth a plug nickel."

Ultimately, the fight had no bearing on Armstrong's legacy. Even without the fourth title, he'd already punched his ticket to boxing immortality.

Henry Armstrong Statistics	
Featherweight Champion	1937–1938
Lightweight Champion	1938–1939
Welterweight Champion	1938–1940
Wins	152
KOs	100
Losses	22
Draws	9
Total bouts	183

Archie Moore was among the most colorful champions of the 1950s.

Archie Moore

Full name:	Archibald Lee Wright
Nickname:	The Old Mongoose
Birthdate:	December 13, 1913; died December 9, 1998
Place of birth:	Benoit, Mississippi

His colorful personality overshadowed the fact that he had one of the best minds in boxing history.

Archie Moore loved being called "The Mongoose." The nickname suited him, he said, because the mongoose killed rats and snakes. Moore thought of himself killing the many rats and snakes in the boxing business.

Journalists of his day usually called him "Ancient Archie," which wasn't an insult but a term of wonderment. A.J. Liebling of *The New Yorker* once compared him to Herman Melville's Ahab, with the heavyweight title serving as Moore's personal Moby Dick. In turn, Moore once sent a note to Liebling and signed it, "The most unappreciated fighter in the world." Moore's complaint was ironic, for he's generally regarded as one of the greatest fighters that ever lived.

Few fighters performed so well for so long, with as many physically demanding bouts, nor continued to excel past the age when most fighters were retiring. For comparison, Joe Louis had retired by October 1951, while Moore, five months older than Louis, was still 14 months away from beating Joey Maxim for the light heavyweight championship. Then, astonishing for a fighter who had won the title when he was near 40, Moore's reign of nine years

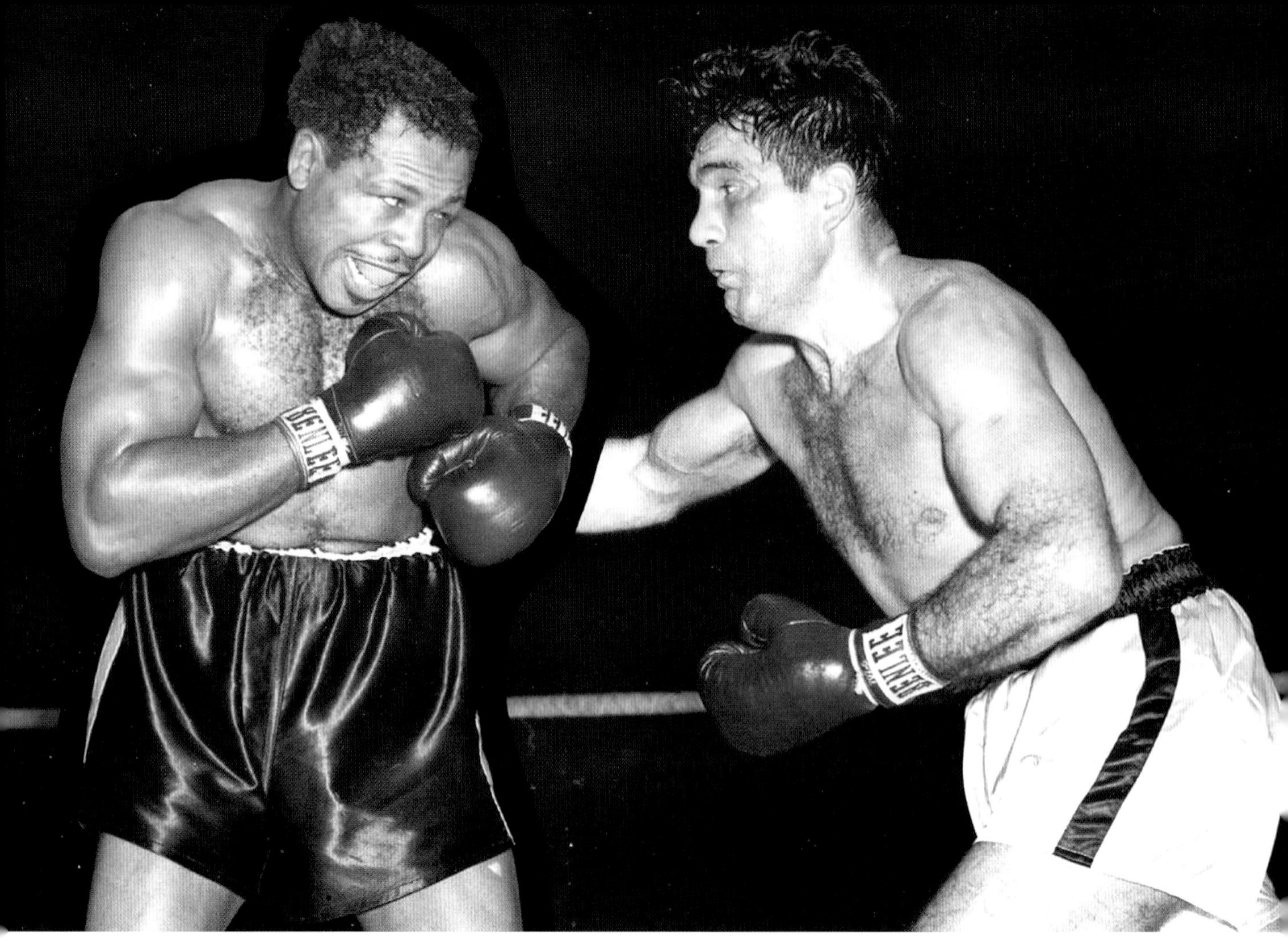

Moore won the light heavyweight championship by defeating Joey Maxim (right) on points over 15 rounds. St. Louis, Missouri, 1952.

and four months was the longest of any light heavyweight champion.

Gray-haired and paunchy, Moore was still dangerous as he approached the half-century mark. Though listed as 45, he was 48 when he stopped young heavyweight contender Alejandro Lavorante in 10 rounds, scored a one-round knockout of longtime rival Howard “Honeyboy” King, and fought a 10-round draw with future light heavyweight champion Willie Pastrano. It wasn’t until a fourth-round TKO loss to young and mobile Cassius Clay – soon to be Muhammad Ali – that Moore thought about quitting. After a farcical knockout of wrestler Mike DiBiase, he never fought again except for exhibitions. Remarkably,

He was old for a fighter, but he was a strong man.

Moore had been a professional boxer from 1935 to 1963, from the Great Depression to the Space Age.

Many have tried to describe Moore's style in the ring, his peculiar cross-armed defense, his penchant for mind games, the way he glared across the ring at opponents, in the words of Budd Schulberg, "like some South Sea emperor staring down an unruly subject." Perhaps the most insightful comments came from Pastrano, who fought the ageless wonder in Los Angeles when Moore was 48 and Pastrano was 28.

For author Peter Heller, Pastrano described the pathetic sight of Moore waddling to the ring. Pastrano pitied him. But in the first round Archie started talking to him, making comments from behind his arms.

"All I see is his forehead and eyes," Pastrano said. "He was behind two big arms like tree trunks, he crossed them in front of him. He would shake one, he called it his 'rattlesnake.'"

In round two Moore whispered to Pastrano, "Stand still."

As if mesmerized, Pastrano did as Moore asked.

Then Moore belted him.

"He used psychology," Pastrano said. "He was a wise old man."

Part of Moore's success was that his wizened look – gray whiskers, an appendix scar, unflattering baggy trunks – distracted from his powerful shoulders and torso. He was old for a fighter, but he was a strong man.

His statistics tell a story of longevity and durability. He took part in 220 bouts, with 186 wins, 23 losses, and 10 draws. His 132 wins by knockout is the highest total by an American fighter. Since contemporary boxers don't fight as often as they did in Moore's time, his knockout record is likely to stand forever. Many came courtesy of his quick right hand punches, though he was just as dangerous with his left.

He'd endured a poor childhood in Missouri, including a stint as a petty thief, but he credited a 22-month term in Boonville State Reformatory for shaping his mind. He read voraciously, learning about heroic figures from the past and thinking of the man he wanted to be in the future. Released from Boonville, Moore eventually went into boxing. His past as a street fighter and some random bouts at the reformatory convinced him he had a gift for punching. "I could knock a guy down any time I got two or three punches together," he said.

Like most Black fighters of the 1930s and '40s, Moore fought wherever he could for very little money. Moore recalled it as a time of traveling by bus and staying in filthy flophouses. He once hopped a train and was attacked by a club-wielding brakeman. The assailant missed and the club splintered, but the event haunted Moore, certain that he'd narrowly missed having his skull "crushed and my brains splattered on the side of that freight car."

He became a regular attraction in San Diego, but much like Jack Johnson had done in an earlier era, Moore spent years battling other Black fighters, including Bob Satterfield, Curtis "Hatchet Man" Sheppard, Jimmy Bivins, Lloyd Marshall, and Holman Williams. The pool of talented Black contenders at 160 and 175 pounds was deep – a Los Angeles promoter once told him that there were too many Black fighters in the city and advised Moore to move on. Though Moore lost three bouts to Ezzard Charles and another to Charley Burley, he gradually established himself as one of the premier talents in an overstocked weight class.

In 1945 Moore aligned with manager Jimmy Johnston, a character known as "The Boy Bandit." Moore's relationship with Jimmy and his brother Charles was prickly, yet they smartened him up to the business. Still, many years passed before Moore was granted a title shot. When he finally won the championship from Maxim in 1952, Moore could barely enjoy it. "It was no big deal to me," he said later, "because it was something I knew I could do."

Moore defeated Maxim twice more by 15-round decision, in Ogden, Utah in 1953, and in Miami in 1954. "He's the best I ever fought," Maxim said after the Miami fight.

His distinctive way with words combined with his big punch made Moore one of the most popular fighters of his time. He seemed to know a little about everything, from bizarre diets to human psychology. There were quirky techniques of his own invention, such as "relaxology," "escapology," and "breathology." Moore served this claptrap to reporters and they loved him. He made their jobs easy.

Moreover, his collection of elegant ring robes, topped off by his trademark mustache, gave him a stunning visual appeal, slightly offbeat but regal. Moore's sartorial taste was a recurring topic, particularly when he was once spotted on New York's Fifth Avenue in a white dinner jacket and Bermuda shorts. Yet there were times when Moore's colorful personality threatened to eclipse his brilliance as a fighter.

Moore had been a professional fighter for seven years when Muhammad Ali was born, and in many ways, he paved the way for Ali. Moore was outspoken, socially conscious, easily the most articulate of fighters. He even dabbled in poetry. He was a showman, and mingled comfortably with politicians and movie stars. "He was one of the greatest, underestimated fighters that ever lived," said Ali, who once sought Moore as a coach. "Underestimated and played down."

Moore with California boxing promoter Onyx Roach, 1956.

Moore was played down because it was easy to label him an aging eccentric. Rare for the time, he didn't allow promoters and boxing organizations to run his career. Many were irked by his treatment of the light heavyweight title, which he defended infrequently.

From the moment he won the light heavyweight championship, Moore coveted the heavyweight crown worn by Rocky Marciano. With greater money to be made in the heavier class, Moore managed a sort of balancing act, taking on heavyweights and campaigning for a shot at that

Moore and Harold Johnson (right) fought each other five times, with Moore winning four.

title. When pressed by the powers that be, he'd boil himself down to 175 and defend his light heavyweight title. Then, his obligation fulfilled, it was back to the heavyweights.

Thanks to his endless lobbying, Moore eventually got his shot at Marciano in 1955 at Yankee Stadium. This bruising, highly dramatic fight got off to a surprise start when Moore knocked Marciano down in the second round. But as most had predicted, the younger, stronger man bashed away at Moore and eventually stopped him in the ninth. Marciano's retirement led to Moore facing Floyd Patterson for the vacated title in 1956. He was knocked out again, this time in five. Moore's heavyweight dream seemed just beyond his reach.

From then on, Moore seemed cavalier about his light heavyweight title, defending it at his convenience and drawing the ire of various sanctioning bodies. He was increasingly viewed as a fast talker and a manipulator. Syndicated columnist Milton Gross spoke for many at the time when he described Moore as a cheeky conman, "who can tell a white lie with such charm that you are bound to accept it even if you don't believe it."

But as Moore fell out of favor, a bout from December of 1958 endeared him to the public all over again. That was the night when Moore's greatness was revealed to all.

Yvon Durelle was a fixture of Canadian boxing with nearly 100 fights on his record. Known as "The Fighting Fisherman," he did most of his fighting in New Brunswick. At different times he was recognized as the "Canadian light heavyweight champion," a distinction that sounded better than "The Fighting Fisherman." Yet Durelle had shown initiative by stepping out of Canada and taking fights in Detroit and New York, resurrecting a flagging career and proving himself to be a rugged, if not especially nimble fighter. Though he'd also acquired the British Empire belt at 175 pounds, Durelle's main selling point was his hard-charging style. He was the perfect television brawler.

After four consecutive wins in 1958, Durelle was matched with

Moore for a title bout nationally televised on ABC TV. The fight would take place in Canada at the Montreal Forum. Ancient Archie was at his buoyant best before the fight, cracking jokes about Durelle and deflecting questions about his age. (Moore's mother had recently told the press that her son was three years older than he claimed, which Moore denied.) Installed as a 13–5 betting favorite, earning near $100,000 against 40 percent of the gate and television money, Moore probably saw his Montreal adventure as an easy night's work.

At this point Moore had scored 126 career KOs and needed one more to surpass the record set by Young Stribling in 1933. Most predicted he'd get that knockout against Durelle. The knockout record, and the fact that it was the first bout televised from Canada, gave Moore–Durelle some minor intrigue, but overall the event was a hard sell. Though getting on in years, Moore was still considered a master at 175. Few saw Durelle as anything more than a brave underdog, a willing brute drafted to be Moore's seventh title defense. That is, until the first round began.

With less than a minute gone, Durelle shot a right hand to Moore's jaw. Ancient Archie went down hard. The sound of his body hitting the canvas echoed across the Forum as if a bass drum had been kicked.

Moore somehow got back to his feet only to be knocked down a second time. Referee Jack Sharkey ruled it a slip, but Moore was clearly hurt. As the woozy veteran rose again, Durelle clubbed him to the canvas for the third time. It surely looked like the end of Moore as he tried to rise, grasping the ropes for support. Few champions had ever been knocked around so badly and not lost their title.

Smelling blood and money, Durelle came banging forward. Amazingly, as Durelle dropped several heavy punches on him, Moore reached into his foggy old mind and summoned up the survival techniques he'd learned during his many years of combat. At round's end Moore was still standing, albeit on legs of rubber.

Moore scored a technical knockout of James J. Parker in the ninth round at Maple Leaf Stadium. Toronto, 1956.

He walked slowly to his corner and sat down. He looked every bit his age, whatever it may have been.

Moore would remember praying during that painful first round. He wasn't asking God for victory, but simply to get his own licks in. "I don't mind losing this fight," he prayed, "but I got to hit this guy some punches."

Moore's manager at the time was Jack Kearns, the former handler of Jack Dempsey. During the 60-second rest, Kearns suggested Moore stand up and wave to his wife and children at ringside. Though dizzy and possibly concussed, Moore did as Kearns asked. Of course, this was calculated so Durelle would see that Moore was feeling fine. Moore wrote in his autobiography, "That Kearns was a smart cookie."

Moore willed himself back into the fight, staying cool during the next few rounds as Durelle tried to line him up for another right hand. Moore appeared to be taking control, but Durelle nailed

Viewers half-expected Moore to grab a chair from ringside and smash it over Durelle's back.

him again in the fifth with a right to the jaw. Moore found himself on the canvas for the fourth time. While the Montreal crowd unleashed a bloodthirsty howl, Moore rose at the count of six. Not wanting to let Moore get away as he had in the first round, Durelle swarmed the older fighter and punched him all around the ring. Incredibly, Moore survived again.

Showing incredible resolve and focus, Moore came back in the sixth and landed several hard blows. To the surprise of the crowd, he even knocked Durelle down at the end of the seventh round. It seemed Durelle was tiring. Durelle wasn't done, though. In the ninth round the burly Canadian dug in for his last stand, trading punches with Moore. Back and forth they went in a round for the ages. By now the fight had gone beyond boxing and had become a Wild West saloon brawl. Viewers half-expected Moore to grab a chair from ringside and smash it over Durelle's back.

The 10th was more of the same, with Durelle throwing his haymakers and Moore stinging him with sharp right leads and combinations. But while Durelle was fighting out of desperation, Moore was composed and landing stiffer shots. Moore scored another knockdown as the round ended, and two more in the 11th. By then, The Fighting Fisherman was finished. To the utter astonishment of the audience, Sharkey counted 10 over Durelle at 0:49 of the round.

Somehow, the Mongoose had come back from the edge of disaster and retained his title. What he did that night in Montreal would be remembered as one of the miracles of boxing history.

"This, I felt, was my finest hour," Moore said years later. So did most everybody else.

The next day's newspapers were flooded with glowing tributes to Moore. Syndicated columnist Joe Williams called the fight "a moving experience," and praised it as "the TV show of the year."

Another angle of Moore's bout with James J. Parker. Toronto, 1956.

Italy's Giulio Rinaldi checks Moore's weight prior to their title bout. Moore went on to win by 15-round decision. New York, 1961.

"This was classic melodrama," he wrote, "replete with physical furies, suspenseful situations and sentimental splendor . . . At times such as these, the rowdy old sport climbs out of the muck and walks with the gods . . ."

It remains the single most discussed fight of Moore's career. Few realize there was a Moore–Durelle rematch the next year, where Moore easily stopped Durelle in three rounds. The first fight, however, was an immediate classic, etched in stone forever.

Yet there was still the issue of Moore's shoddy treatment of the light heavyweight championship. Authorities grew tired of Moore defending the title when it suited him, or dismissing ranked contenders as "unqualified." By 1961 Moore was under fire for not defending against top contender Harold Johnson, never minding that he'd already defeated Johnson in four out of five bouts. Eventually, the National Boxing Association and then the New York State Athletic Commission withdrew recognition of Moore as the 175-pound titlist. The European Boxing Union followed suit. Moore didn't retire immediately, but by 1964 he'd phased himself out of boxing.

Moore stayed busy by acting in movies and TV shows and as a public speaker. He served occasionally as an adviser to fighters, including George Foreman, but Moore devoted most of his time to working with youth groups and anti-drug abuse programs.

Moore died in 1998, leaving behind his wife, Joan, and four children. His age was still debated. By the year given by his mother, Moore was 84. "My mother should know," he once said. "She was there. But so was I. I have given this a lot of thought and have decided that I must have been three when I was born."

It is now generally accepted that 1913 was the year of Moore's birth. Ring historians still quibble over it, though, just as they do over his exact number of fights. That's probably how Moore wanted it. He liked to keep you guessing.

Then he'd belt you.

Archie Moore Statistics	
Light Heavyweight Champion	1952–1962
Wins	186
KOs	132
Losses	23
Draws	10
No-contests	1
Total bouts	220

Dignified and mild-mannered, Joe Louis was an American icon.

Joe Louis

Full name:	Joseph Louis Barrow
Nickname:	The Brown Bomber
Birthdate:	May 13, 1914; died April 12, 1981
Place of birth:	Chambers County, Alabama

During his long reign as heavyweight champion he seemed to be carrying the fate of a nation on his back.

On a Wednesday night in June 1938, Max Schmeling of Germany entered the ring at Yankee Stadium to battle the heavyweight champion, Joe Louis. Unlike any fighter before him, Schmeling had been fitted with a cloak of international villainy. While fascism and political unrest spread across Europe, he symbolized the foreign menace. Louis, suddenly cast as America's redeemer, coolly waited for the fight to begin.

Black fans had idolized Louis since the beginning of his career. White Americans had also invested in Louis, since he represented the stars and stripes against Schmeling, the idol of Nazi Germany. Schmeling was uninterested in politics, but the Nazi propaganda machine had proclaimed him a figure of Aryan superiority, while the American press labeled Schmeling an "Adolph Hitler booster." With war in the air, Louis–Schmeling II became much more than a sporting event. As *Radio Guide* reported in the week before the contest, the fight would "hold two continents breathless."

Louis was aware of the Nazi angle, but for him the fight was more personal. Schmeling had defeated Louis two years earlier, handing him the only

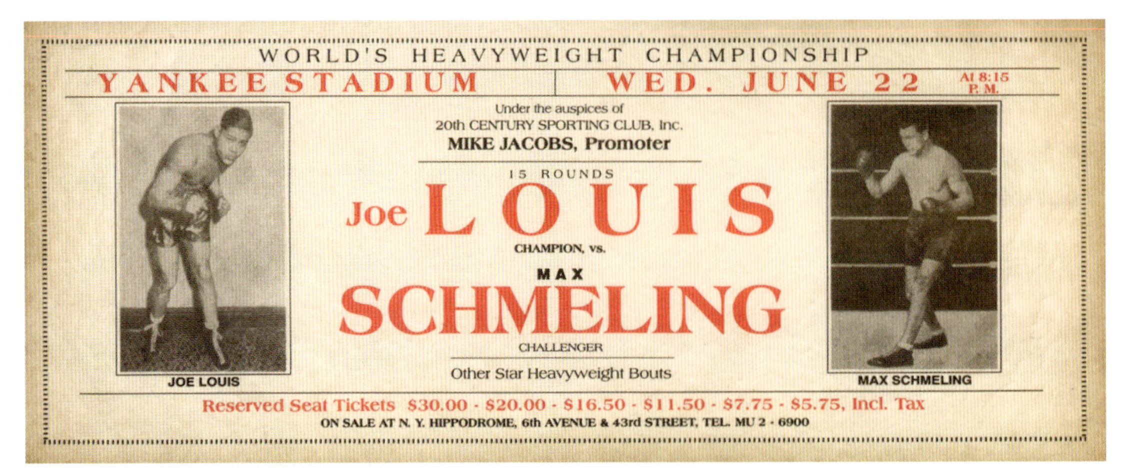

The second Louis–Schmeling bout stirred emotions around the world.

loss of his professional career to that time. On that previous night in 1936, Schmeling noted a flaw in Louis's stance that allowed him to be hit with right hands. From this minor observation, Schmeling gave Louis a methodical battering and knocked him out in the 12th round. Louis's growing fan base was heartbroken. One year later, when Louis defeated James J. Braddock for the championship, he told reporters to not call him "champ" until he avenged the loss to Schmeling.

Louis admitted that he'd taken Schmeling lightly the first time, and that fame had gone to his head in those early days of his career. Now, for the rematch, he was focused. One reporter described Louis in the moments before the first bell being as calm "as an executioner about to throw the switch on a condemned man."

Louis spent a half-minute measuring Schmeling, stalking him. Then he pounced. Two years of coiled vengeance came forth as Louis unloaded on Schmeling with both hands. The German was helpless, stuck along the ropes as Louis pounded him. At one point Schmeling turned to the audience in Yankee Stadium and howled like a trapped animal. It was later revealed that one of Louis's blows had fractured a bone in Schmeling's spine.

After only 124 seconds, Schmeling lay on the canvas. Louis

had knocked him down three times. A white towel fluttered in from the fallen challenger's corner, a sign of surrender.

Louis's lightning quick victory sent the country into a kind of delirium. There were riots reported in Cleveland, Chicago, and elsewhere, with celebrations in Black neighborhoods turning unruly and requiring police intervention. There were reports of people listening to the NBC radio broadcast and dropping dead from heart attacks. There were shootings, car crashes, and all manner of mayhem. A reporter claimed to have visited Harlem that night, watching hundreds of revelers dance around a coffin draped in a Nazi flag.

After the quick destruction of Schmeling, Louis told the press, "Now you can call me champ." It was his greatest moment.

In retrospect, Louis's victory that night grew into a sort of American touchstone. It was as if Louis had knocked out not only Schmeling, but also Hitler and the entire Third Reich. Never again would such international importance be attached to a mere boxing event.

Joseph Louis Barrow was born in La Fayette, Alabama, on May 13, 1914. His family was part of the southern Black migration north, which resulted in Louis growing up in Detroit. His father had been a sharecropper in the South, but was later committed to an insane asylum where he eventually died. His father's condition haunted Louis. "You don't forget a thing like that," he said.

Louis was a teenager when he gave up violin lessons to embark on an amateur boxing career. He turned pro at 19, managed by a pair of Black businessmen, John Roxborough and Julian Black. They were numbers runners, with connections in the Chicago fight scene.

Completing the team was trainer Jack "Chappie" Blackburn, a former fighter who'd done prison time for murder. It was purportedly Blackburn who helped Louis develop his hard-punching style. Blackburn felt a Black fighter wouldn't win many decisions against white fighters, so he encouraged Louis to get close to an opponent and destroy them with short, compact punches. Like a thunderbolt crackling through the heavyweight division, Louis knocked out 19 of his first 23 opponents.

Among Louis's early wins were brutal stoppages of former champions Primo Carnera and Max Baer. These bouts were major New York happenings, convincing promoter Mike Jacobs that Louis was an important new attraction. The Louis–Baer bout had earned a million dollars at the gate, something unheard of in the middle of the Great Depression.

Moviegoers of the time became accustomed to watching newsreel footage of Louis in action. The images were mesmerizing. At 6'1", and just under 200 pounds, Louis was lithe for a heavyweight, with power in both hands. The sight of him taking a few shuffling steps to corner a victim before releasing his quick, devastating punches became embedded in the public consciousness. Seeing him projected on the screen of a dark movie house, often in slow motion, gave Louis a larger than life, dreamlike feel. Opponents fell before him in odd ways, their twisted and flailing bodies reflecting the impact of Louis's punches.

White fans may have preferred a white champion, but they appreciated Louis's ability. Unlike the abrasive Jack Johnson, Louis was reserved and polite. Also, society had changed a bit since the days of Johnson, and most of Louis's fans hadn't even been born when Johnson was active. Black fans idolized him; white fans respected him. He quickly became the most talked about fighter in the country, as well as the most famous Black man.

Even the music industry caught on. Within months of Louis beating Baer, radio listeners heard a new song by Joe Pullum, "Joe Louis is the Man." In 2001, musicologist Rena Kosersky released a compact disc featuring 15 songs about Louis, telling *The New York Times* she'd located at least 43 recordings about him, including one by Count Basie's Orchestra. Most were recorded between 1935 and 1940.

Louis fascinated the press, though writers relied on handy stereotypes, presenting Louis to readers as a childlike Black man with the fighting instincts of a jungle animal. It took a few years for writers to depict Louis as he really was, a quiet young man and a serious practitioner of boxing. In the meantime Louis kept knocking opponents out.

James Braddock had won the heavyweight championship in 1935, his own story providing inspiration for newspaper readers. He was "The Cinderella Man," a washed-up journeyman who had emerged from a janitor's job to win one of the most revered titles in all of sports. Yet Cinderella stories must end when the clock strikes 12. For Braddock, Louis represented midnight.

Jacobs convinced Braddock to fight Louis by arranging one of the sweeter deals in boxing history. If Louis won, Braddock would receive a small percentage of Louis's ring earnings for as long as he remained champion. Though the actual percentage varies depending on the source, the gist was that Braddock would get a piece of Louis's money. But he would earn it the hard way.

Louis bombards Schmeling. New York, 1938.

A crowd of approximately 45,000 filed into Chicago's Comiskey Park on June 22, 1937, most expecting to see the crowning of a new champion. Braddock was game, but Louis cut

Harlem revelers after a Louis victory. 1935.

him to shreds and knocked him out in the eighth with a perfect right to the jaw. "When he knocked me down," Braddock said, "I could have stayed there for three weeks."

Louis was 23, the youngest man to win the heavyweight title at the time. He was only the second Black fighter to win the heavyweight crown, and as was often the case when Louis fought, there were Black celebrations around the country. Author Richard Wright once described the street festivities after a Louis fight as having a "religious feeling . . . a feeling of unity, of oneness."

No fighter had ever meant so much to America's Black population. Yet Louis said he felt strange when Black fans would grasp his hand and say, "You're our savior." In a short time he'd gone from being the savior of boxing, to the savior of his people. Against Schmeling he'd represented oppressed people everywhere versus the symbol of Nazi strength. This would be a burden on any young man. When Louis visited the White House during this period, President Franklin D. Roosevelt greeted him as a kind of demigod and grabbed his right arm. "Joe," the president reportedly said, "we're depending on those muscles for America." As Louis wrote in his 1978 memoir, "The whole damned country was depending on me."

After Louis defeated Schmeling in 1938, the heavyweight class was thin on quality contenders. Journalists grew bored with Louis's easy knockout victories, and dubbed his challengers the "Bum of the Month Club." Most were paralyzed with fear at the thought of facing Louis. "I remember in 1940 I walked Johnny Paycheck into the ring against Joe," said trainer Ray Arcel, "and his knees were actually trembling."

Still, there were some memorable fights in between the blowouts. The best of them came in June of 1941. Billy Conn, the great light heavyweight out of Pittsburgh, boxed beautifully for 12 rounds before Louis finally stopped him at 2:58 of the 13th. The dramatic bout called for a rematch, but Japan's attack on Pearl Harbor that same month stalled everything in America, including boxing. By the spring of '42, Louis had reported for military duty.

Against Schmeling he'd represented oppressed people everywhere versus the symbol of Nazi strength.

He was more celebrity than soldier, an amiable goodwill ambassador visiting military camps and putting on boxing exhibitions. There was an incident in Alabama where an MP harassed Louis and Sugar Ray Robinson because they were standing in the "whites only" section of an Army bus station. The result was an order to end segregated buses in Army camps. It was a small victory for Louis, and a sign of his standing. The image of Louis in uniform seemed to encourage Americans as the war drudged on, as did his famous quote: "We'll win because we're on God's side." By the time of his release from the service in October of 1945, Louis was a full-fledged American hero. *New York Post* columnist Jimmy Cannon's line about Louis being "a credit to his race – the human race," became Louis's unofficial branding.

Louis's long-awaited return to boxing was planned by Mike Jacobs for June of 1946 at Yankee Stadium. The promoter chose Louis's old rival, Billy Conn, as the homecoming champion's first challenger after the war. It was a rematch five years in the making.

Capturing the tone of the day, Louis–Conn II was the first heavyweight championship bout broadcast on television, a sign of things to come in fast moving post-war America. It was also significant because of something Louis said during the prefight buildup. When asked about Conn's speed in the ring, Louis introduced a phrase that would become part of the American lexicon: "He can run but he can't hide."

Thanks to Jacobs' inflated ticket prices and the nation's appetite for a big fight, Louis's return generated a near $2 million gate. But even though Louis won by a knockout in the eighth round, the fight was disappointing. Both men looked sluggish, their reflexes dulled by their time away from boxing. Most of the criticism was heaped on Conn, but Louis looked bad, too. Yet the champion's problems were due to more than mere ring rust.

Though his demeanor was somber and low-key, Louis liked to party. He was a gambler, a free spender, and despite being married was involved with some of the most beautiful women in show business. Because the press respected him, Louis's personal dramas were only hinted at in the newspapers. Yet there was an increasing sense that the world's most celebrated fighter had money problems and a troubled personal life.

By the end of 1948 Louis had endured two difficult bouts with Jersey Joe Walcott, a journeyman who'd once been the champion's sparring partner. The crowd at Madison Square Garden jeered the first, a 15-round split decision for Louis. Many thought Walcott had deserved the verdict, but that Louis had been awarded the decision because of his stature. Always dangerous in rematches, Louis met Walcott a second time at Yankee Stadium and scored an 11th round KO. He'd erased the doubt created by their first match, yet Louis knew he was not the fighter he'd once been. He was a tired man.

Louis launches a right hand against a bloodied Cesar Brion. Louis won by 10-round decision. Chicago, 1950.

Louis retired as champion at age 34, but his mounting financial problems brought him back.

Louis retired as champion at age 34, but his mounting financial problems brought him back in 1950 to challenge the new champion, Ezzard Charles. Louis lost by 15-round decision, but he continued boxing until October of 1951.

The end for Louis came in Madison Square Garden when he suffered a disastrous knockout loss to a young contender, Rocky Marciano. In the eighth round, when Marciano smashed Louis through the ropes onto the ring apron, a generation wept. Louis went over backwards, wrote Jimmy Cannon, "like someone who sits on a window sill and falls out when the pane breaks." The referee didn't bother with a count.

As Louis was helped to his feet, a cloud of sadness settled over the arena. Even Marciano was upset. The gloom was partly because Louis's epic career was finally over. It was also because no one knew what would become of him now.

Louis's main problem was with the Internal Revenue Service. The issue stemmed from two fights in 1942 just prior to his entering the service. A good American, he'd donated his pay from each event to the Army and Navy relief funds. Yet Louis's patriotism backfired, as the IRS claimed he'd never paid taxes on the money. The government added interest to the penalties each year, along with more penalties, until Louis was buried in debt. "When that income man said one million," Louis said, "I stopped listening."

He spent the 1950s and '60s working in a variety of jobs – professional wrestler, casino greeter, boxing promoter, spokesman for the Cuban Tourist Commission – and at one point was even hired by Muhammad Ali as an "adviser." Still, Louis's financial hole only grew deeper. Even the Black culture seemed to abandon Louis in favor of edgier personalities such as Malcolm X and the highly politicized Ali.

Adding to Louis's problems was his increasing use of cocaine. Stories surfaced of a coke-fueled Louis

Louis's image was often used to inspire Americans during the Second World War.

barricading himself in hotel rooms in fear of mysterious gangsters. He eventually sought help for his addiction, though the man who emerged after rehab was hardly the champion of old. Louis was deteriorating mentally and physically.

Silenced by a series of strokes, Louis spent his final years in a wheelchair, living on the charity of friends and celebrities. He died on April 12, 1981, at age 66. He was buried in Arlington National Cemetery, a resting place for war heroes.

Louis left behind some remarkable statistics, including a record of 68-3, with 54 knockouts. He'd reigned as heavyweight champion for 11 years and eight months, or 4,270 consecutive days, the longest title reign in history. He'd made 25 successful defenses of the title, a record for a single reign that may never be surpassed. *The Ring* magazine named him Fighter of the Year in 1936, 1938, 1939, and 1941.

Yet his boxing achievements were only part of the Louis story. His death reminded people of how he'd broken down the color barrier in sports. Older sportswriters looked back with bittersweet nostalgia, ashamed that more wasn't done for Louis during his difficult years.

The passing of Louis was especially sad for Max Schmeling. The pair had become friendly since their two historic bouts. Schmeling had quietly helped pay Louis's medical expenses and also sent a sizable check to his widow. "Joe was a boxing genius," Schmeling said.

There was an oft-repeated legend that involved a young Black convict in 1935. He'd died in a North Carolina gas chamber. As the fumes overtook him, he had supposedly gasped, "Save me, Joe Louis!" It wasn't true; it was a myth created by a journalist. Yet the story was repeated as gospel and appeared in many Louis biographies. That it seemed plausible is due to the strength of Louis's image. There was a time when it seemed he was here to save people. How many fighters can we say that about?

Left: Monument to Joe Louis, known also as The Fist located in Detroit, Michigan. Dedicated on October 16, 1986. Right: U.S. Congressional Gold Medal for Joe Louis.

Joe Louis Statistics	
Heavyweight Champion	1937–1949
Wins	68
KOs	54
Losses	3
Draws	0
Total bouts	71

Sugar Ray Robinson brought glamor to boxing, and reigned supreme for most of two decades.

Sugar Ray Robinson

Full name:	Walker Smith Jr.
Nickname:	Sugar Ray
Birthdate:	May 3, 1921; died April 12, 1989
Place of birth:	Ailey, Georgia

With a fabled career full of remarkable achievements, the original "Sugar Ray" is still regarded as the best of all time.

Very little film exists of Sugar Ray Robinson in his prime. This is one of the shames of boxing history.

The available footage is proof enough that he was extraordinary – graceful on his feet, bold, throwing fast combinations – yet he's already a 30-year-old middleweight. There is scarcely any filmed record of Robinson in his 20s as a shimmering fast welterweight.

He was born Walker Smith Jr. in Ailey, Georgia,on May 3, 1921. Legend has it that his father's drinking caused the family to splinter. Walker was uprooted to Detroit, and then, at age 10, to Harlem. He earned money by tap dancing outside Broadway theaters, but by his teen years he was hooked on boxing. In Detroit he'd idolized an older kid who boxed. That kid happened to be Joe Louis.

In New York, Walker Smith evolved into a promising amateur boxer. Too young at 14 for an Amateur Athletic Union (AAU) card to verify his amateur status, Smith's trainer, George Gainford, gave him the card of another boy who no longer boxed, a fellow named "Ray Robinson." Later, when a reporter told Gainford, "That's

Robinson wallops his arch-rival, Jake LaMotta. Chicago, 1951.

some sweet fighter," someone nearby shouted, "Sweet as sugar." Thus, Sugar Ray Robinson was born.

By 1940 Robinson was an amateur sensation, winning the New York Golden Gloves at lightweight. At age 18 the *New York Daily News* dubbed him, "pound for pound, the best amateur fighting man in America." The term "pound for pound best" would follow Robinson for the rest of his life and long after his death.

It did no good to compare Robinson to other fighters. It was more appropriate to place him next to great musicians or artists, such were his skills at improvising against an opponent. Fritzie Zivic, who lost twice to him, said in 1970 that Robinson was nearly perfect in the ring. "I mean, the fellow was a great boxer, great puncher, could take a punch, and could move," Zivic said. "What more do you need for a fighter? His hands look like they go off automatically. You couldn't take a chance with him."

Just under six-feet tall, slender, with slick hair and a trim mustache that gave him a debonair look, Robinson was grace and style personified. Crowds would gather just to watch him skip rope. But for all his poise, what drew the most attention to Robinson was his ability as a puncher. He was dangerous with both hands, and he had what was known in the business as "killer instinct." Unique among fighters, Robinson could land devastating blows while moving backwards, his hands firing so quickly that rivals never saw the punch that scrambled their senses.

His credentials say a lot. He was the welterweight champion from 1946 to 1950. From 1951 to 1958 he won the middleweight championship a record five times. He was *The Ring* magazine's Fighter of the Year in 1942 and 1951, and received the same distinction from the Boxing Writers Association in 1950. *The Ring* editor, Nat Fleischer, who'd observed boxing since the 1900s and noisily declared his preference for fighters of the distant past, admitted in 1958 that Robinson "would have stood out in any era."

From the time he turned professional in 1940 at age 19, to his 30th birthday in 1951, Robinson's record was 124-1-2, with victories over the top welterweights and middleweights of the day. The only man to defeat Robinson in his prime was the notorious "Bronx Bull," Jake LaMotta.

At the time of the first Robinson–LaMotta meeting in October of 1942, Robinson was an undefeated 21-year-old who had beaten just about every welterweight available but was idling while waiting for a shot at the champion, Freddie Cochrane. Promoter Mike Jacobs recognized Robinson's talent but was reluctant to put him in the championship picture. Joe Louis was already a dominant champion at heavyweight, and Jacobs doubted paying customers would get behind another dominant Black fighter at welterweight. Jacobs wanted to keep the welterweight title "fluid."

"He told me he wanted to have two or three guys fighting for it," Robinson said, "because there was more money in it that way. I understood that. It was just good business."

> Robinson was one of the few fighters unwilling to go along with the whims of racketeers.

Moreover, Robinson already had a reputation for being difficult. Jacobs imagined Robinson would only grow more egotistical if he won the championship. When Cochrane joined the navy during WWII, the welterweight championship remained frozen for nearly three years.

Another issue that delayed Robinson's march to the title was the presence of low rent gangsters who had infiltrated the business. Robinson was one of the few fighters unwilling to go along with the whims of racketeers. He wouldn't take dives or bribes. With unbridled confidence, Robinson did things his way. Even when Robinson occasionally agreed to carry a mob-owned fighter, he'd sometimes forget the deal and knock the guy out. It is doubtful that another fighter could accomplish as much as Robinson did under such stifling conditions or defy the mob with such fearlessness.

When Robinson talked about testing the middleweight class, Jacobs matched him against LaMotta at Madison Square Garden. LaMotta was a burly 20-year-old middleweight, a crowd pleaser. Robinson won by 10-round decision, but the fight was competitive enough that a rematch was held at Detroit's Olympia Stadium in February 1943. This time LaMotta won on points, handing Robinson his first loss as a professional. The rubber match was held in the same venue three weeks later. Robinson's hand was raised after 10 rounds. Again, the fight was close. Fans booed the decision.

Like Robinson, LaMotta was also dealing with gangsters who

Robinson trains while accompanied by a full jazz band.

wanted to control his career. With LaMotta and Robinson stifled by unfair obstacles (and Cochrane stationed at Pearl Harbor), one of their options was to keep fighting each other. They fought in New York again in February 1945, and then in Chicago later that year. Robinson won both times by decision. As was always the case when they fought, the customers got their money's worth.

What made the Robinson–LaMotta rivalry so appealing was that it was a classic matchup between a boxer and a brawler. This pairing of styles has always enticed boxing fans. There's something exhilarating

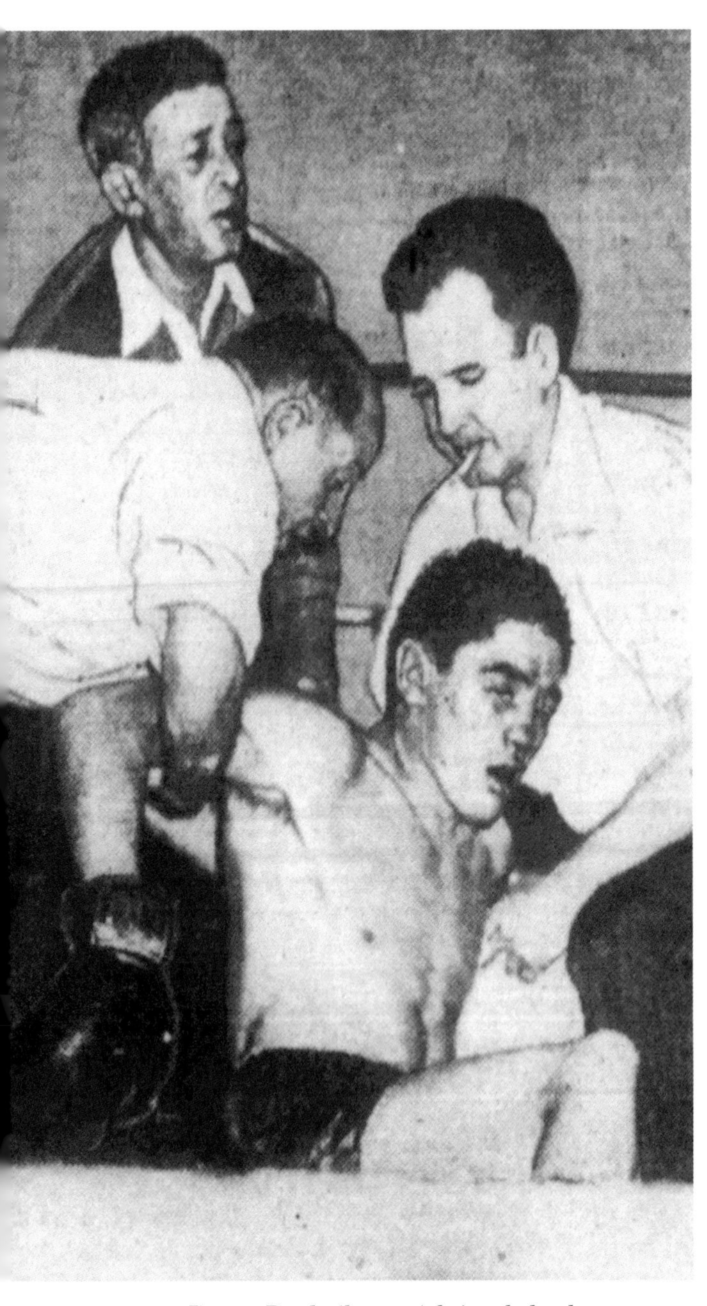

Jimmy Doyle (bottom) being helped up from the canvas by three unidentified men following his match against Sugar Ray Robinson. Doyle died hours later in a Cleveland hospital.

about a quick man using his skills against the brawler (though LaMotta was crafty in his own right, and not merely a thug). Conversely, there's a kind of catharsis that occurs when the brawler beats down the scientific fighter. Sometimes an audience enjoys seeing brains win out. Sometimes, though, they'd rather see brains *beaten* out. Robinson versus LaMotta was the ultimate showcase of brain versus brawn, a dancer versus a slugger.

"I would have to say Robinson was the best I fought – a cutie, fast, with all the tricks, but he could also take a punch and he could throw one," LaMotta said.

Robinson eventually won the welterweight title in 1946 by beating Tommy Bell on points in New York. Five years and five title defenses later, as he had physically outgrown the 147-pound class, he challenged for the middleweight title. Fate must've been a boxing fan, because by then LaMotta had finally won the middleweight belt. The boxing world braced itself for Robinson–LaMotta VI.

The fight, which came to be known as "The St. Valentine's Day Massacre," took place in Chicago Stadium on February 14, 1951. The early rounds were competitive, but by the eighth Robinson was punishing LaMotta with terrible blows to the ribcage and face. By round 11, LaMotta looked like the walking dead, shambling toward Robinson with lifeless eyes, kept up only by a primordial instinct to keep fighting. It ended in the 13th with LaMotta on the ropes, nearly out on his feet, saved from disaster by referee Frank Sikora. In stopping LaMotta, Robinson won the middleweight title and ended the rivalry that defined his career.

Robinson had his share of lows, including a controversial Army hitch where he went AWOL and was ultimately discharged, leaving some to label him a deserter. It took a few fights for Robinson to get back into the good graces of the public.

There was also a tragic night in Cleveland where Robinson's opponent, Jimmy Doyle, died after being knocked out. Prior to the bout Robinson dreamed that he had killed Doyle. Robinson was so bothered by the omen that he tried to postpone the fight. Convinced to go on with the bout, Robinson was horrified to see his nightmare realized. "I stood over him," Robinson wrote in his autobiography, "transfixed, seeing my dream come true, horribly true."

Robinson grew increasingly uncomfortable with his profession. "I've never enjoyed boxing," he once said. "It's just a business with me."

But if he disliked his vocation, he certainly loved the things he could buy with his earnings.

Robinson owned most of a city block in Harlem. His businesses included a barbershop, a restaurant, a real estate office, and a dry cleaners. He even bought a lingerie store for his loyal wife, Edna Mae. Robinson lived large. The locals cheered him as he drove around the neighborhood in his flamingo pink Cadillac convertible. The elegant champ in his fuchsia automobile represented the height of success for a Black man in America, circa 1950.

The centerpiece of Robinson's fiefdom was a plush nightclub

known simply as "Sugar Ray's." The venue hosted some of the top entertainment figures in the area and was often used by Robinson as a headquarters, a place for press gatherings and important announcements. It was also a hotspot for certain Harlem gangsters; it has been speculated that Robinson's friendship with a prominent Black crime figure kept him from undue interference from the Italian mob.

Robinson was also known for his entourage, a noisy group that included his personal barber, a dwarf, a chauffeur, and a fellow hired simply to whistle "Sweet Georgia Brown" while the champion skipped rope. Like a king and his attendants, Robinson rarely traveled without his flunkies.

Shortly after beating LaMotta, a tour of Europe led Robinson to London where he lost a surprise 15-round decision to Randolph Turpin. Robinson regained the title two months later in New York at the Polo Grounds, scoring a dramatic TKO at 2:52 of the 10th. Bleeding from a cut over his eye and desperate to win, Robinson maneuvered Turpin to the ropes and threw dozens of punches; the sheer frenzy of the finish showed how badly he wanted the title back. Robinson's victory kicked off a jubilant night in Harlem, reminiscent of the times when Joe Louis or Jack Johnson won an important fight.

Wanting a title in a third weight class, Robinson took aim at light heavyweight champion Joey Maxim. In September of 1952, on a steaming hot night in Yankee Stadium, Robinson was winning on points when he succumbed to the heat. It was shocking to see a limp and dehydrated Robinson helped out of the ring after the 13th round, the only time in his career where he failed to finish a fight.

Robinson surprised his fans in January of 1953 with his retirement from boxing. He spent the next two years trying to reinvent himself as an entertainer, but supper club crowds quickly grew tired of his rudimentary tap dancing and off-key singing. By 1955 he was boxing again.

The comeback was rough for Robinson. He struggled through a

Robinson knocks down Jean Wanes during a non-title bout. Zurich, Switzerland, 1951.

handful of bouts and even dropped a 10-round decision to journeyman Ralph "Tiger" Jones. Still, audiences remained captivated by him.

"There's a quirk in American hero worship," said journalist Jack Newfield, "that I think people love you more if you've been humbled once or twice, if you seem vulnerable, if you have a weakness. I think the same thing is true of Robinson. After he lost a couple of times, when he reached a level of being a mere mortal, not a god, then I think he became more and more popular."

On December 9, 1955, 35-year-old Robinson entered the ring at Chicago Stadium as a 3–1 underdog and challenged middleweight champion Carl "Bobo" Olson. Summoning the old magic one more time, Robinson knocked Olson out in the second round and regained the championship. He cried with relief for several minutes after the bout, one of the rare times Robinson

In the second defense of his welterweight title, Robinson knocked out Chuck Taylor in six rounds. Detroit, 1947.

showed such emotion. In a rematch, Robinson KO'd Olson in four.

Thus began a whirlwind period for Robinson. First he engaged in two bouts with Gene Fullmer where he lost and then regained the championship. Robinson's fifth-round KO of Fullmer to reclaim the title in 1957 was noted for the left hook that ended the fight. Crisp and quick and right on the chin, it was hailed forever in boxing lore as the "perfect punch." Then Robinson lost and regained the title again, this time against rugged Carmen Basilio. The two Basilio bouts were action packed 15-round split decisions, each voted Fight of the Year by *The Ring* magazine in 1957 and 1958.

By now Robinson had won the middleweight title five times. He'd also amassed a fortune thanks to his stubborn negotiating tactics, which now included his demand for percentages of the television rights and closed-circuit theater screenings. His cut for the second Basilio bout was more than the entire players' share of the 1958 World Series. Yet promoters complained that it cost so much to pay Robinson that they rarely made money for themselves. Surprisingly, attendance for Robinson–Basilio II had been below expectations. The press began portraying Robinson as money-obsessed, arrogant, and past his prime.

After beating Basilio, Robinson was inactive for several months, negotiating for a bout with Archie Moore that never came off. For failing to defend the title, the National Boxing Association withdrew recognition of Robinson as champion in March 1959, though New York still considered him the titleholder. In 1960 he lost his remaining portion of the title to Paul Pender by a split decision in Boston. There was a rematch, but Robinson lost again by split decision. Seeing Robinson struggle with the brittle-handed Pender was a sign that his career had turned a corner. He'd never be champion again.

Robinson fought on until 1965. These were unpleasant times; he lost as often as he won. During his final year of activity he turned 44 while fighting 17 times in a 12-month

Whether Robinson was the best fighter of all time is rarely questioned. It's hard to imagine another fighter in the top spot.

span. After a 10-round decision loss to Joey Archer in Pittsburgh, Robinson retired for good. "No more comebacks," he said.

Madison Square Garden organized a farewell tribute for Robinson, but as he took his bows and enjoyed a lengthy standing ovation, his smile concealed the fact that his life was crumbling. Due to Robinson being abusive and unfaithful, his marriage to Edna Mae had ended in a sour divorce. Desperate for money, he'd already started selling his Harlem businesses. The IRS was coming to carve him up.

Robinson tried to resurrect his show business career, but the best he achieved were a few bit roles. He married again and started a foundation for underprivileged children, but by the 1980s he began showing the effects of his old profession: slurred speech, a faulty memory. Ravaged by Alzheimer's, diabetes, and heart ailments, he died in 1989 at age 67.

His professional record is astounding, standing at 174-19-6, with 109 knockouts. Most of his losses came after the age of 40. As an amateur, he lost only a few times in approximately 90 contests.

Nothing on his ledger was a cultural landmark on par with Dempsey–Tunney II, or Louis–Schmeling II, but Robinson was the biggest boxing draw of the 1950s. He fought in just about every major American venue and was also an attraction in Europe. His rematch with Turpin drew more than 61,000 to the Polo Grounds – it earned close to a million dollars, at the time a record gate for a non-heavyweight bout – while his fight with Maxim brought nearly 48,000 to Yankee Stadium. If Robinson didn't quite attract the audiences of Dempsey or Louis, it was because ticket buyers generally preferred the heavyweights. But those who followed Robinson were treated to a kind of perfection offered by neither Dempsey nor Louis. Robinson was flawless. No one fought like him.

Whether Robinson was the best fighter of all time is rarely questioned. It's hard to imagine another fighter in the top spot.

Contemporary fighters earn larger paydays and therefore don't have to fight as often, so it is unlikely anyone will match Robinson's 174 wins, nor his 109 knockouts. With the added weight classes and belts available now, a fighter isn't likely to lord over one division and win the title five times, as Robinson did at middleweight.

Additionally, we'll never see a fighter with Robinson's versatility. It is a rare fighter who can move as well as he did, and also punch with such precision, the left hook short and compact, the overhand right coming down like a scythe. It is doubly rare to see a fighter switch from classic boxing to suddenly become a snarling street fighter. Robinson could do it.

True, he fought too long. Yet even those who saw Robinson in his final years of competition were lucky. They'd witnessed slivers of a talent that appears once in a century.

Sugar Ray Robinson Statistics	
Welterweight Champion	1946–1951
Middleweight Champion	1951, 1952, 1955, 1957, 1958
Wins	174
KOs	109
Losses	19
Draws	6
No-contests	2
Total bouts	201

The Will o' the Wisp, Willie Pep.

Willie Pep

Full name:	Guglielmo Papaleo
Nickname:	Will o' the Wisp
Birthdate:	September 19, 1922; died November 23, 2006
Place of birth:	Middletown, Connecticut

Plagued by a weakness for gambling and the worst accusations that can befall a fighter, Willie Pep was history's greatest featherweight.

Of all the boxing legends spread out over a century or more, Willie Pep laid claim to one of the most peculiar, in that he once allegedly won a round without throwing a single punch. Pep claimed it happened, and one journalist vowed that he'd been there the night Pep supposedly did the impossible.

The fight in question took place at the Minneapolis Auditorium in 1946. Pep's opponent was local favorite Jackie Graves, stopped by Pep in the eighth round. The legend goes that Pep made an off-air remark to radio commentator Don Riley, something about winning a round without hitting his opponent. Riley dared him to try and suggested he do it in the third.

More than 20 years passed before Riley mentioned the fight at a boxing banquet. Riley disclosed that Pep had indeed spent the third round slipping and feinting, controlling the action without landing so much as a glancing blow. Riley then claimed to have spied the scorecards. To his delight, the judges had penciled Pep's name next to round three. There was some mystery as

Pep was masterful against France's Ray Famechon. Pep won by 15-round decision. New York, 1950.

to why Riley hadn't mentioned Pep's stunt before, but once the story was out it caught on like a grass fire. Pep mentioned it in a 1970 interview. He said he didn't hit Graves but spent most of the three minutes, "making him look so bad they gave me the round."

When the esteemed Red Smith of *The New York Times* heard of the incident and described it in one of his columns, the effect was extraordinary. With Smith's endorsement, Pep went from being a well-liked boxing figure to something almost supernatural.

He'd been a dancing devil of a fighter, a sprite of the ring nicknamed "The Will o' the Wisp." He could turn almost any opponent into an unwilling partner in a game of "catch me if you can," though the prize for catching Pep was usually a quick jab to the mouth. From the time he won the New York version of the featherweight championship from Chalky Wright in 1942, Pep was viewed as a wunderkind. A mere 20-year-old, Pep befuddled the more experienced Wright for 15 rounds, faking him out of his boots with tricky steps and counters. He was, wrote W.C. Heinz, "the greatest creative artist I ever saw in a ring."

Pep seemed unsolvable. He won 62 consecutive fights before venturing into the lightweight class where he met Sammy "The Clutch" Angott. Pep was sampling the 135-pound class, a bad idea since he was small even for a featherweight. Angott was a mauler who liked to clinch opponents and stifle them from throwing punches. This was a successful strategy against Pep, like trapping a moth under a paper cup. Angott won a 10-round decision but there was no call for a rematch; the fight had been drab, and Pep didn't belong in the lightweight class. Moreover, Angott was on the downhill side of his career and would lose several of his upcoming fights. Pep, meanwhile, continued to soar.

In the three-year period after the fight with Angott, Pep dominated a gallery of top featherweights, including Sal Bartolo (three times), Jackie Wilson (twice), Manuel Ortiz, Phil Terranova, Jock Leslie, and Chalky Wright (three more times). He also served short stints in the Army and the Navy, discharged by both due to an injured eardrum.

Pep made yearly defenses of the featherweight title to satisfy the boxing authorities, but he was usually on the road, fighting non-title bouts throughout New England and along the east coast. He was unusually popular for a featherweight, constantly setting attendance records in one city or another. But no matter how busy he was, Pep always made room on his schedule for bouts in Hartford, Connecticut, which is where it all began for a skinny shoeshine boy named Guglielmo Papaleo.

He was born in Middletown on September 19, 1922. Tired of being harassed for the money he earned shining shoes and selling newspapers, Pep and a friend took up boxing at a Hartford gym. Hartford was a boxing city. Fans were so rabid that promoters ran shows featuring local amateurs fighting under assumed names for money.

When Pep was a 15-year-old flyweight, he was booked to fight in Norwich against a tall featherweight from New York. This turned out to be Ray Robinson, who was already an accomplished amateur. The matchup of two future greats was hardly memorable. It took place in one of Norwich's makeshift fight venues, what Pep called "the attic of a big shed." Robinson won on points. Noting Robinson's edge in size and experience, Pep said in 1970, "I had no business being in the same ring with Robinson that night."

Still, boxing consumed Pep's existence. He spent less time at school and more time learning the fine points of the ring. Pep credited trainer Bill Gore with making him into a great fighter. Pep was a nervous type, but Gore taught him to stay calm and cool in the ring. This led some journalists to describe Pep as bland, unemotional. Indeed, compared to the showbiz glamour of Robinson, Pep was a church mouse. His style, the elite footwork, the quintuple left jab, was for the aficionado, not the rabble in the cheap seats.

Though Gore encouraged him to be clever in the ring, Pep could take a man out with a well-placed punch. The rumor was that Pep preferred to beat rivals on points, but if he knew of a good dice game going on somewhere, or he wanted to catch an early train home, he'd step in with a clean shot and end the fight quickly.

Sometimes he'd score a knockout just for emphasis. When Sal Bartolo earned recognition as featherweight champion from the National Boxing Association, Pep put his New York title on the line against Bartolo's NBA title. Answering the question of who the real featherweight boss was, Pep broke Bartolo's nose, broke his jaw, and stopped him in the 12th. When he found himself having to face Wright for the fourth time, Pep knocked him out in round three. "I didn't punch hard," Pep once said, "but I punched often."

Pep's career nearly ended in January 1947 when an airplane he was on crashed in a forest in Millville, New Jersey. Noting his shattered ankle and two damaged

Pep blasts Sandy Saddler on his way to a 15-round decision win. New York, 1949.

vertebrae, doctors feared Pep wouldn't fight again. Six months later he returned, winning a 10-round decision over Victor Flores in the Hartford Auditorium. He resumed his busy schedule, winning against such prominent names as Teddy "Redtop" Davis and Paddy DeMarco.

Pep had been featherweight champion for nearly six years when he faced Sandy Saddler in Madison Square Garden on October 29,

1948. Saddler, a 5'8" contender who was three inches taller than Pep and punched like a middleweight, stopped Pep at 2:28 of the fourth round. Saddler's upset victory sent tremors through the boxing world. Pep admitted he had underestimated Saddler, and that it was becoming difficult to prepare himself for fights.

In February of 1949 Pep and Saddler returned to the Garden for a rematch. To the astonishment of the crowd, Pep used his experience and cunning to win a 15-round decision and regain the title. It wasn't easy. He suffered horrible cuts on his face, and after the bout he needed to be helped from the ring. "Pep's mouth was a puffed mass," reported the *Buffalo Courier*, "but through it he managed a gargoylish smile of victory."

It had been a cruel contest, with rough tactics from both men. But even in this backstreet type of fight, Pep was brilliant, outmaneuvering a taller, younger, and stronger opponent. "He was light as a ballet dancer," noted the *Courier*, "as he circled in, out and around the sometimes bewildered Saddler." When Saddler put on a late rally and had Pep hanging on, there was still a feeling in the Garden that Pep was pulling off an incredible comeback, limping to the finish, but still an absolute master of the ring. "That was the greatest night of my life," Pep said. "I realized how great it was to be champion again. And I knew I won it from a good fighter."

Pep seemed to have regained his old form. Among his title defenses in this second reign was a 15-round points win over the popular French featherweight, Ray Famechon, in New York in 1950. After the bout Famechon was heard muttering to himself in French, words that translated roughly to, "I couldn't hit him because I couldn't find him."

But Pep's second turn on the mountaintop was short-lived. There were two more bouts with Saddler, grueling events that saw Pep surrender in his corner each time, once because of a damaged shoulder and then because of an eye injury. These two bouts were marred by fouling from both men, but it was Pep who took the most criticism for being a dirty fighter. The press also labeled him a quitter. He objected to the printed attacks, but his reputation was sagging. His status plunged further after embarrassing knockout losses to Tommy Collins in 1952, and Lulu Perez in 1954.

The Perez fight, in particular, which saw Pep KO'd in two rounds at Madison Square Garden, plagued him for years to come. The sight of Pep losing in such a manner was peculiar. He was hit with punches he usually avoided, and the way he fell drew suspicion. Moreover, a last-minute influx of betting money swung the odds wildly in favor of Perez. Many were convinced the fight was "in the bag" for Perez and that Pep was taking a dive. Though some viewed his bad showing as simply proof of Pep's advancing age, others were dubious that he would fall so easily to the lightly regarded Perez. The *New York Mirror* referred to the Pep–Perez bout as "the big dumper," while Lester Bromberg of the *New York World-Telegram and The Sun* noted Pep's three trips to the canvas as "unnecessarily theatrical tumbles."

"My wives were great housekeepers. After the divorces they all kept the house."
– Willie Pep

The state commission dismissed the talk of a fixed fight, but barred Pep from fighting in New York again. The given reason was concern for his health. It may also have had to do with his suddenly negative reputation. Pep denied the fight was shady. The commission's banning of him, he later wrote, was only "sour grapes" from people who'd bet on him.

Still, Pep kept fighting. He had a trail of broken marriages behind him, each one more costly than the one before. "My wives were great housekeepers," he said. "After the divorces they all kept the house." Pep was also struggling with a lifelong gambling habit, which included him being hauled before a Hartford judge nearly a dozen times on illegal gambling charges. "Slow horses and fast women," was

Pep slips a punch from Chalky Wright and lands his own jab in return. Pep won the featherweight title from Wright in 1942.

Pep's usual response when asked about his shrinking bank accounts.

A knockout loss to Hogan "Kid" Bassey in 1958 marked the end of Pep as a serious moneymaker. He retired in 1959 but made a pitiful comeback in 1965 at age 42. Now he was a boxing drifter, fighting for meager paydays in remote places. Once, at a weigh-in in Arizona, an opponent asked for Pep's autograph.

Pep maintained his humor during his fallow period, but there was a sense of melancholy to him. He once told *Sport* magazine that, "fame is fleeting. Who'll remember us? Just the kids in our era. Fathers will know us but their kids won't." Pep retired again after losing a six rounder in Virginia.

The stats he left behind, however, are staggering. Pep scored 229 wins, against only 11 losses and one draw, with 65 wins by knockout. He boxed a total of 1,955 rounds. During his two reigns as featherweight champion he made 10 successful title defenses, winning nine by KO, proof that he hit hard when the occasion called for it.

Floyd Mayweather Jr. earned acclaim in more recent years for retiring with a record of 50-0. Yet Pep was 62-0 before he lost to Angott and ran off an additional 73 fights without a loss before losing to Saddler. Mayweather's record is respectable, but Pep surpassed it twice in one career. Prior to the first bout with Saddler, Pep was 134-1-1. (The only opponent he drew with was Jimmy McAllister in Baltimore. In a rematch, Pep KO'd McAllister in two. Again, Pep could punch when he had a point to make.)

Pep was *The Ring* magazine's Fighter of the Year in 1945, while his first bout with Wright was chosen as *The Ring's* Fight of the Year for 1942. His dramatic win over Saddler was given the same award in 1949. In 1994 Pep received an award for meritorious service from the Boxing Writers Association. In 1999 the Associated Press named Pep the greatest featherweight of the 20th century.

In Pep's later years he worked as a referee and served as a deputy inspector on the Connecticut boxing commission. He appeared to be surviving.

“Maybe he wasn’t as colorful as Sugar Ray, but Willie was smarter.”
– Freddie Brown

Controversy struck when *Inside Sports*, a magazine known for tabloid sensationalism, published a story in 1980 called “The Fix,” about an old-time champion who threw a fight in 1954. Though Pep wasn’t named, he felt the story was about him and Perez. Pep believed the article hurt his reputation, and that he was passed over for the state commissioner’s job because of it. He filed a $75 million libel suit against Newsweek Inc., but a six-person jury voted against him.

Fortunately for Pep, history was kinder to him than the jury. Among boxing fans there was a nostalgia boom for fighters of the past, and Pep’s name took on a new kind of reverence. Some even rated him above Robinson. Paul Pender, a middleweight champion of the early 1960s, once said Robinson “couldn’t shine Willie Pep’s shoes as far as pure boxing ability. Willie Pep would be in back of you, beside you, making you miss punches, pat you on the fanny as you went by. Ray Robinson couldn’t do that.” Freddie Brown, a respected boxing trainer whose career dated back to the 1940s, was more succinct: “Maybe he wasn’t as colorful as Sugar Ray, but Willie was smarter.”

Sandy Saddler once claimed to have seen Pep do the unimaginable against Chalky Wright in 1944. According to Saddler, Wright had been chasing Pep all night and finally had him trapped in a corner of the ring. “Chalky cocked his right to throw a bomb,” said Saddler, “and Pep ducked through his legs and got away. That’s right. Pep ducked right through Chalky’s legs . . . I never forgot that. It was the damndest thing I’d ever seen.”

Then there was the time Pep won a round without throwing a punch. That was everyone’s favorite Pep story, even if was increasingly doubted.

In 2003, researcher Jake Wegner turned up an old article from the *Pioneer Press*. For Pep’s cult of admirers, Wegner’s find was a shock. What he discovered was no less than an original fight report filed by journalist Joe Hennessy. From ringside, Hennessy described the third round of Pep–Graves as a whirl of violence from both fighters. "A clicker couldn't count the blows," Hennessy wrote.

Was Pep's punchless round a lie?

Riley and others discredited Hennessy, while some accepted Wegner's find as proof the story had been phony. Some even accused Riley and Pep of concocting it together.

Could Pep win a round without landing a punch? Could anyone? The myth's longevity is a credit to Pep. If anyone could pull off such a thing, it would've been Will o' the Wisp.

Pep carried in his wallet a frayed and yellowed clipping of an article about the Graves fight. He also kept photocopies of it in his desk at the commission office. Out of 241 fights, that one gave Pep his identity. He loved showing the article to people, as if proving that he was, once, truly magical. When he died at 84 in a Connecticut nursing home in 2006, chances are he still had a copy in his wallet.

Pep knew the truth: Fighters pass away. Legends live forever.

Willie Pep Statistics	
Featherweight Champion	1942–1948, 1948–1950
Wins	229
KOs	65
Losses	11
Draws	1
Total bouts	241

Marciano began his reign as heavyweight champion by knocking out Jersey Joe Walcott. Philadelphia, 1952.

11

ROCKY MARCIANO

Full name:	Rocco Francis Marchegiano
Nickname:	The Rock, The Brockton Blockbuster
Birthdate:	September 1, 1923; died August 31, 1969
Place of birth:	Brockton, Massachusetts

With his rough style, courage, and mild manner, Rocky Marciano personified America's image of the brave, humble champion.

He was smallish for a heavyweight. His amateur experience was minimal. He didn't begin his professional career in earnest until he was nearly 25. Indeed, only the most optimistic would've earmarked Rocky Marciano for success.

He simply didn't look the part. He was clumsy, with short arms, and the thick legs of a football lineman. His hair was thinning, and he had the drowsy demeanor of a bored doorman at a nightclub. When veterans of the business learned that Charley Goldman, one of the most esteemed trainers of the day, had taken Marciano on as a reclamation project, they laughed.

Marciano was an ex-GI who had boxed in the service. He'd only taken it up after learning the boxing team was excused from kitchen duties. Since then, he'd participated in some amateur tournaments and had fought a few times as a pro, but he looked raw. It was only when he landed a punch that Goldman's interest made sense. The most jaded observers could see that the awkward little guy had a mysterious and rare power, the kind that only a few fighters possess, the

A sad sight. Marciano defeats the aged Joe Louis. New York, 1951.

sort that sent men spinning across the ring. "The punch," Goldman said, "is a shortcut to the money."

He didn't look like much, but a generation of boxing fans would soon think all fighters should look like Rocky Marciano.

He would come to embody the bruised and bloodied fighter, behind on points, willing to take a few punches in order to land one, pulling victory out of the fire with one last, desperate right hand. When people thought of Marciano, they thought of his stubborn courage and toughness. They thought of violence. "As did few other fighters of his time," wrote Ed Fitzgerald of *Sport*, "Rocky satisfied the primitive bloodlust that lured the customers through the doors."

He was born Rocco Marchegiano on September 1, 1923, in Brockton, Massachusetts, a small city 20 miles south of Boston. For Rocco, the dreary life promised by Brockton in those days was unappealing. He'd watched his father toil for years at one of the city's many shoe factories, but after a few factory stints of his own, Rocco knew he wanted something different. After his Army years he'd tried to make it in baseball. It was only after a failed tryout with the Chicago Cubs that he considered boxing. He'd had some success in the Army tournaments. His fists were like clubs.

Marchegiano had a solid amateur career in New England, but Boston promoters weren't interested in him. Eventually he caught the attention of Al Weill, a well-connected New York matchmaker who introduced him to Goldman. Weill told him to shorten his name. Goldman shortened his punches. Still, boxing was in a poor state in 1948–49, with television draining the life out of live gates. No one was betting on the newly minted "Rocky Marciano" to lift it out of the gloom. He was just another Italian fighter, of which there were many at the time.

Sometimes Marciano and a friend would hitchhike to New York to work with Goldman. After a particularly uncomfortable ride in the back of a cabbage truck, Goldman claimed the two looked "like they'd come down to sweep the place up."

When Goldman first met him, Marciano was throwing his right hand like a thief heaving a brick through a store window. Goldman taught him to throw the punch properly, and to always follow it up with a left. This was basic stuff, but Marciano learned. Goldman recognized Marciano's determination and liked what he saw. He dubbed Marciano's right hand "Suzy Q."

Marciano's first significant coverage came after his second New York bout. On December 30, 1949, he knocked out Carmine Vingo in six rounds. Marciano didn't celebrate, for Vingo was immediately hospitalized with a brain injury. As Vingo clung to life at St. Clare Hospital in the Bronx, New York papers ran morbid photos of him on the canvas, the nearly lifeless result of Marciano's punches. Scary headlines appeared for consecutive days as Vingo remained on the critical list. The deathwatch was on.

Marciano felt terrible about injuring his opponent and was photographed praying for Vingo in a Brockton church. The fact that an Associated Press photographer just happened to be there made the photo seem contrived. Still, the image of Marciano looking saintly as he knelt in prayer was dramatic. It was *cinematic*. The accompanying stories emphasized the "sickening impact" of Marciano's punch. It was in this way that newsreaders learned about this previously unknown fighter. The image was marketable: the young Italian boxer was as powerful as a tank, but big-hearted, and close to God. No publicity team could've designed a better introduction of Marciano to the public. Best of all, Vingo lived.

Marciano received more widespread coverage in the fall of 1951. He was matched against the beloved former champion, Joe Louis, at Madison Square Garden. The faded, 36-year-old Louis entered the ring as a slight betting favorite, only to crumple before the younger man's power. Marciano knocked him out in the eighth round. "I'm glad I won," Marciano said, "but sorry I had to do it to him."

As the public mourned the end of Louis's career, Marciano was hailed as the bright new star of the business. By now he was undefeated in 38 consecutive bouts, and his earnest manner had made him a likable, marketable commodity. He was shy, soft-spoken, an all-American Italian guy. His past as a GI helped, since most of the people watching him on television or listening on the radio were ex-GIs as well. Also, like most of his fans Marciano was newly married and planning a family. Reporters from the top magazines and newspapers portrayed him as a glowing symbol of post-war American success, a regular Joe making his way.

But if it was easy to call Marciano a great guy, writers were less compelled to call him a great fighter. He was forever deemed "crude" and "unpolished." Getting by on

"The Rock" displaying the tools of his trade.

his strength earned him the same sneers as an actor who gets by on his looks. Rather than fully investing in Marciano, journalists labeled him a work in progress and lumped him in with the other young heavyweights of the day – Roland La Starza, Rex Layne, and Harry Matthews. He eventually beat them all, but the press still hesitated to praise Marciano as anything more than a street fighter with connections.

Even Marciano's fans were scrutinized, as if unwelcome. They were often depicted as unruly hooligans, as unsophisticated as their ring idol. A.J. Liebling once described a Marciano cheering section as "unsavory young yokels with New England accents."

The press was unanimous, however, in praise of Goldman. Most Marciano stories focused on the old ring Svengali who had turned a fighter

Marciano's supporters always turned out to celebrate his victories. Brockton, 1952.

of limited skills into a contender. An eccentric former bantamweight, Goldman had been mentoring fighters since 1914. With his black bowler cocked over one eye and his thick Brooklyn accent, he fit the press's image of a grizzled boxing lifer. No trainer was ever credited for a fighter's success as was Goldman for the reign of Marciano. It was as if Goldman were Michelangelo chiseling a fighter from a block of marble, the press waiting like cynical connoisseurs for the finished work.

Of course, Marciano was much better than anyone knew. He

absorbed what Goldman taught him and trained feverishly. Few athletes were better conditioned than Marciano. Fewer still were as hungry for money and recognition. The dread of becoming an anonymous figure in a Brockton factory drove Marciano to train hard and absorb Goldman's every lesson.

By September of 1952, when Marciano fought heavyweight champion Jersey Joe Walcott in Philadelphia, he was as good as he'd ever be. That was fortunate because 38-year-old Walcott was a wily champion, as crafty as anyone in the business. Unexpectedly, Walcott knocked Marciano to the canvas in the first round – a shock for Rocky's fans, who'd never seen him down before – and then put him through one of the most grueling bouts on record. "It was a messy fight, bloody and oddly glorious," reported Jimmy Cannon of *Newsday*.

It appeared Walcott was going to keep the title until the dawn of the 13th round, when Marciano finally herded him into a corner and landed a crushing right to the jaw. "It was one of the most stunning blows ever seen," reported *The Buffalo News*, describing the sound of the punch as "a deathly, terrible noise." Walcott didn't fall immediately but deflated on the spot, like a giant parade float that had been punctured by a bullet. Ten seconds later there was a new champion.

The Marciano loyalists, who'd come to Philadelphia from all corners of Massachusetts and Rhode Island, rushed the ring. "A horde of wild-eyed rooters pushed past the police," wrote the Associated Press, "swarmed through and over the press rows and stormed into the ring to pay homage to their hero." The ring became so jam-packed that Marciano's admirers began falling out, hurting themselves on the chairs and tables below, like bodies tumbling from a burning building. Surrounded by a phalanx of police, Marciano shot out of the chaos and ran back to his dressing room at a fast trot.

With the retirement of New York Yankees star Joe DiMaggio in 1951, Marciano stood to become the country's premier Italian sports hero. Not as urbane as the famous centerfielder – one couldn't imagine Rocky sweeping Marilyn Monroe off her feet as DiMaggio would do – he offered something different, something earthy. At the time, the heavyweight champion was still regarded as a figure of major importance, the toughest man in the land. A memorable photograph of the period shows Marciano and DiMaggio with President Eisenhower during a special White House event. The president and DiMaggio are admiring Marciano's fist, held out like a cinderblock for their amusement.

The journalists of the day could no longer deny Marciano. He was still viewed as an unskilled and occasionally dirty fighter, but they also saw him as a respectable champion who wore the crown with pride, the fruition of the Italian immigrant experience. And in Brockton he was royalty.

With the retirement of New York Yankees star Joe DiMaggio in 1951, Marciano stood to become the country's premier Italian sports hero.

Few cities had ever embraced a champion the way Brockton embraced Marciano. On the night he won the title, police estimated 25,000 people had overtaken Brockton's downtown area, a gathering larger than the city's V-J Day celebration at the end of the war. The Marciano victory parade reportedly drew between 60,000 and 100,000 people, more than had come out when Presidents Roosevelt and Truman visited the city.

Marciano would defend the heavyweight championship six times over the next three years. There was a rematch with Walcott where the ex-champion seemed to give up in the first round; an 11th round TKO over La Starza, who had nearly beaten Marciano a few years earlier and deserved a rematch; a 15-round decision over the gallant Ezzard Charles at Yankee Stadium; a rematch with Charles at the same location where the challenger inflicted a terrible gash on Rocky's nose, only to be beaten into submission in the eighth; a ninth-round knockout of England's Don Cockell in San Francisco; and his final bout, a ninth-round knockout of the cunning light heavyweight champion Archie Moore.

Marciano retired seven months after the Moore bout. He was 32. His given reason was that his wife, Barbara, wanted him to spend more time with his family. Yet other reasons were hinted at over the years, everything from disagreements with his manager Al Weill, to Goldman's suggestion that Marciano had peaked and would soon go into decline. It was also said that Marciano was tired of the Spartan regimen required to be a boxer. Boxing, he would say, was a "lonely existence."

Yet Marciano looked miserable at the New York press conference announcing his retirement. The sadness may have come from his decision to give up not only the title, but also his identity. "What could be better," Marciano once said, "than walking down any street in any city and knowing that you are the champion?"

Marciano slugs it out with Ezzard Charles. New York, 1954.

The Ring magazine had chosen Marciano as Fighter of the Year in 1952, 1954, and 1955, putting him in a rare group of three-time winners. *The Ring* also gave Fight of the Year nods to his first bout with Walcott (1952), his defense against LaStarza (1953), and his second bout with Charles (1954). The Boxing Writers Association selected him as Fighter of the Year in 1952. In 1954, Marciano was named Athlete of the Year by *Sport* magazine, a surprise to many considering Roger Bannister had broken the four-minute mile that year, and baseball's Willie Mays had another sensational season.

Trainer Charley Goldman (right) stands next to Marciano after another victory. Chicago, 1953.

The height of Marciano's popularity was his 1955 bout with Moore, which drew 61,574 fans to Yankee Stadium. It fell just short of a million-dollar gate, which would've been the first since Louis–Conn II nine years earlier, and doubly impressive in the era of televised boxing. When other factors, including the closed-circuit receipts, were considered, Marciano–Moore cracked $2 million.

Marciano's retirement led to the expected discussions of his place in boxing history. His ranking was uncertain. Marciano's record, 49-0

The Ali–Marciano computer fight of 1969 was one of the strangest events in boxing history.

with 43 knockouts, was unique. Fighters rarely left the business undefeated. To his critics, Marciano received too much credit for beating aged, weather-beaten fighters such as Louis, Walcott, Charles, and Moore. But to Marciano's followers, undefeated meant the same as unbeatable. His admirers were fiercely protective of his legacy and seemed to love Marciano beyond reason. Those who dismissed him did so too easily.

The image projected by Marciano during his retirement was that of the celebrity ex-champion mixing breezily among movie stars and other famous athletes. He made money on the banquet circuit, appearing all around the country for speaking engagements. Tales of his generosity were legendary. If Marciano was booked somewhere and learned Joe Louis or Willie Pep needed money, he'd cancel and send Louis or Pep in his place.

Yet Marciano was restless. His life became a routine of hotels and travel and moneymaking schemes. His home life soured.

In 1969 Marciano took part in a project with Muhammad Ali. Supervised by radio producer and promoter Murray Woroner, the two sparred for a camera crew in a Miami warehouse, miming scenarios that had been determined by a computer. The filmed sessions were cut into three-minute rounds and booked into movie theaters as a special event billed as *The Super Fight*. The computer supposedly picked Marciano to

In the years since Marciano's death, revelations have included everything from his being an extreme womanizer to his having underworld connections.

win by TKO in the 13th, so that's what audiences saw, with Ali dramatically, and unconvincingly, sagging to the canvas.

Though Marciano was middle-aged and wearing a cheap hairpiece that kept sliding off during the filming, Ali praised him as a rough, tough fighter, a great champion. Theater audiences roared when the cartoonish affair ended with Marciano standing over the fallen Ali. That is, the white audiences roared. Black fans were less impressed.

Newspapers treated the simulated fight as a major event. Photos of the brash, young Ali in defeat unleashed a wave of nostalgia for Marciano. It came at a time when rural America might've loved seeing the soft-spoken ex-GI beat up on Ali, the loudmouthed war protester. It was the sort of cathartic show biz for which boxing had always been suited.

Marciano never saw the computerized showdown. In August of 1969, on the eve of his 46th birthday, he was killed in a plane crash in Iowa.

In the years since Marciano's death, revelations have included everything from his being an extreme womanizer to his having underworld connections. There were weird stories of Marciano being frugal to the point of paranoia, allegedly burying his money in various secret locations. Investigative reporter Mike Stanton dug up Marciano's old military records and found that Marciano's superiors had dismissed him as a conniving type given to petty crimes and violence. Even if only half the tales were true, it was apparent that Marciano wasn't as clean living as suggested by the old magazine profiles. Still, the Marciano myth held steady. His younger brother Peter once discussed Rocky's misdeeds with author Russell Sullivan: "Was he a perfect man? No. But again, who is?"

As Marciano's era recedes into history, the temptation is to use him as a portal into the 1950s. He remains the humble champion, the rugged symbol of post-war American strength. He's often presented like a specimen from a simpler, more innocent time, but there was nothing simple or innocent about him or his time. The miracle of Marciano is that he was a man of voracious appetites, for food, for women, for action. Yet for seven years he behaved like a monk and ascended to the heavyweight championship. It's doubtful that Charley Goldman could have gotten a similar commitment from anyone else.

As for Goldman, he died at age 80 in 1968. The rumor was that he died alone in a New York rooming house, found dead with one of Rocky's old robes covering him. The tale was untrue, but journalists liked keeping Goldman and Marciano together. Things seemed better that way.

Rocky Marciano Statistics	
Heavyweight Champion	1952–1956
Wins	49
KOs	43
Losses	0
Draws	0
Total bouts	49

Charismatic and controversial, Ali was the best-known athlete in the world for several decades.

MUHAMMAD ALI

Full name:	Cassius Marcellus Clay Jr.
Nickname:	The Greatest, The Louisville Lip
Birthdate:	January 17, 1942; died June 3, 2016
Place of birth:	Louisville, Kentucky

Refusing the military draft for religious reasons, Ali became an iconic figure and one of the most famous men in the world.

He called himself "The Greatest," but always said it with a twinkle in his eye.

Muhammad Ali was called many other things in his long career. Like the fastest heavyweight who ever lived, the most recognized face on the planet, and one of the key Black figures of the 20th century.

No athlete in any other sport was as revered throughout the world as this colorful Kentuckian. Ali's fame dwarfed that of other athletes. People in the most primitive corners of Earth idolized him.

Born Cassius Clay on January 17, 1942, Ali enjoyed a reasonably stable upbringing in a calm Louisville neighborhood. The incident that altered the course of his life occurred when he was 12 and reported to a local policeman that his bicycle had been stolen. Officer Joe Martin felt sorry for the youngster and introduced him to boxing. Young Clay went on to establish himself as a top amateur boxer and won a gold medal at the 1960 Rome Olympics.

Playful at times, deadly serious at others, one never knew how he might perform in any given contest. He might give you the "Ali shuffle," he might toy with

Ali's handlers go wild after he stops Sonny Liston in one round. Maine, 1965.

you, or he might cut you to pieces. Joe Bugner, who fought him twice and served as his sparring partner in the early 1970s, recalled the anxiety of being in the ring with Ali. "When you're actually fighting him," said Bugner, "it becomes a bit of a terror."

Standing 6'3" and weighing a statuesque 210 pounds in his prime, "The Louisville Lip" was quicker than any heavyweight before him.

"Clay's speed of foot is almost breathtaking," reported the *Detroit Free Press* in 1965. "He's here, there, then he's gone."

Or as the fighter himself said in the most memorable of his many poems, "Float like a butterfly, sting like a bee, you can't hit what you can't see . . . "

Unique among heavyweights, Ali carried his hands low, shooting his jab while circling the ring, leaving opponents frustrated as they pursued him. Rather than duck to avoid punches, he leaned back, gliding out of range. He rarely hit opponents in

His right hand was a slashing blur, thrown somewhat like the right lead of his idol, Sugar Ray Robinson.

the body, preferring to target their faces. "I'm a headhunter," he said early in his career. "Keep punching at a man's head and it mixes his mind." His right hand was a slashing blur, thrown somewhat like the right lead of his idol, Sugar Ray Robinson. He was often criticized for lacking power, but after he'd KO'd the iron-jawed Oscar Bonavena in 1970, Norman Mailer described Ali's punch as "a wrecking ball from outer space."

The accolades are immeasurable. Ali was the first fighter to win the heavyweight title three times. He was *The Ring* magazine's Fighter of the Year six times, and six of his bouts were selected as *The Ring's* Fight of the Year (records in both categories). He appeared on the cover of *Sports Illustrated* 40 times, a figure surpassed only by Michael Jordan, and was *SI*'s Sportsman of The Year for 1974. He dined with presidents and kings. He earned more money than any fighter before him, and had more words written about him than just about any American figure you could name.

Yet all these achievements are mere footnotes in the Ali saga. Even his final record, 56-5 with 37 knockouts, feels insignificant within the framework of his life.

His early persona was a mashup of different poses: the comical bragging of professional wrestling's Gorgeous George; the bombast of rock 'n' roll's Little Richard; the sass of Black comedians on the chitlin' circuit. He boasted that he was pretty, and that boxing would die without him. He gave his opponents nicknames ("The Bear", "The Rabbit", "The Mummy"), wrote insulting poems about them, and predicted with uncanny accuracy the round in which they'd fall. He was funny, impish. He was a rarity in boxing, a lighthearted character in a dangerous business.

He was a 7–1 underdog when he challenged the intimidating Sonny Liston for the heavyweight championship in 1964. Liston quit in his corner before the seventh round. "I AM the greatest," Clay yelled to the spectators in Miami. "I shook up the world!" It appeared there was more to this brash young man than anyone had imagined.

In the rematch, Liston fell in the first round from a punch no one saw, a blow known in history as the "phantom punch." Though many felt something phony had occurred, the cocky new champion went on to make eight consecutive title defenses. He looked more impressive with each outing. When Ali dismantled Cleveland Williams in three rounds at the Houston Astrodome in 1966, the *New York Daily News* called it, "a virtuoso performance." Boxing's young court jester had grown into a fierce ruler.

Yet there were controversies around the champion's personal life. When he announced his alliance with the Nation of Islam, he alienated much of his white audience. When he revealed that his new Muslim name was "Muhammad Ali," there were constant issues with reporters and opponents still calling him "Clay." When Ali refused his induction into the U.S. Army at the height of the Vietnam War, he became the most polarizing figure in all of sports. For defying the government, he was stripped of his boxing license in 1967 and barred from fighting.

Unable to box, Ali went on the lecture circuit. He spoke at colleges and appeared on talk shows, offering a mix of fiery Muslim rhetoric and anti-war talk. To his detractors, Ali was un-American. To his supporters, the government's treatment of Ali was unconstitutional.

It wasn't until October of 1970 that Ali was licensed to fight again. He scored a third-round TKO of Jerry Quarry in Atlanta, but the fight was over so quickly that few could judge how much Ali had lost during his years away. But if Ali's speed had diminished, he'd gained something else. He was now bigger than boxing. He was an anti-establishment icon, a Black idol who had objected to the war on religious grounds and challenged the system.

Meanwhile, a new champion had emerged in Ali's absence, a rugged

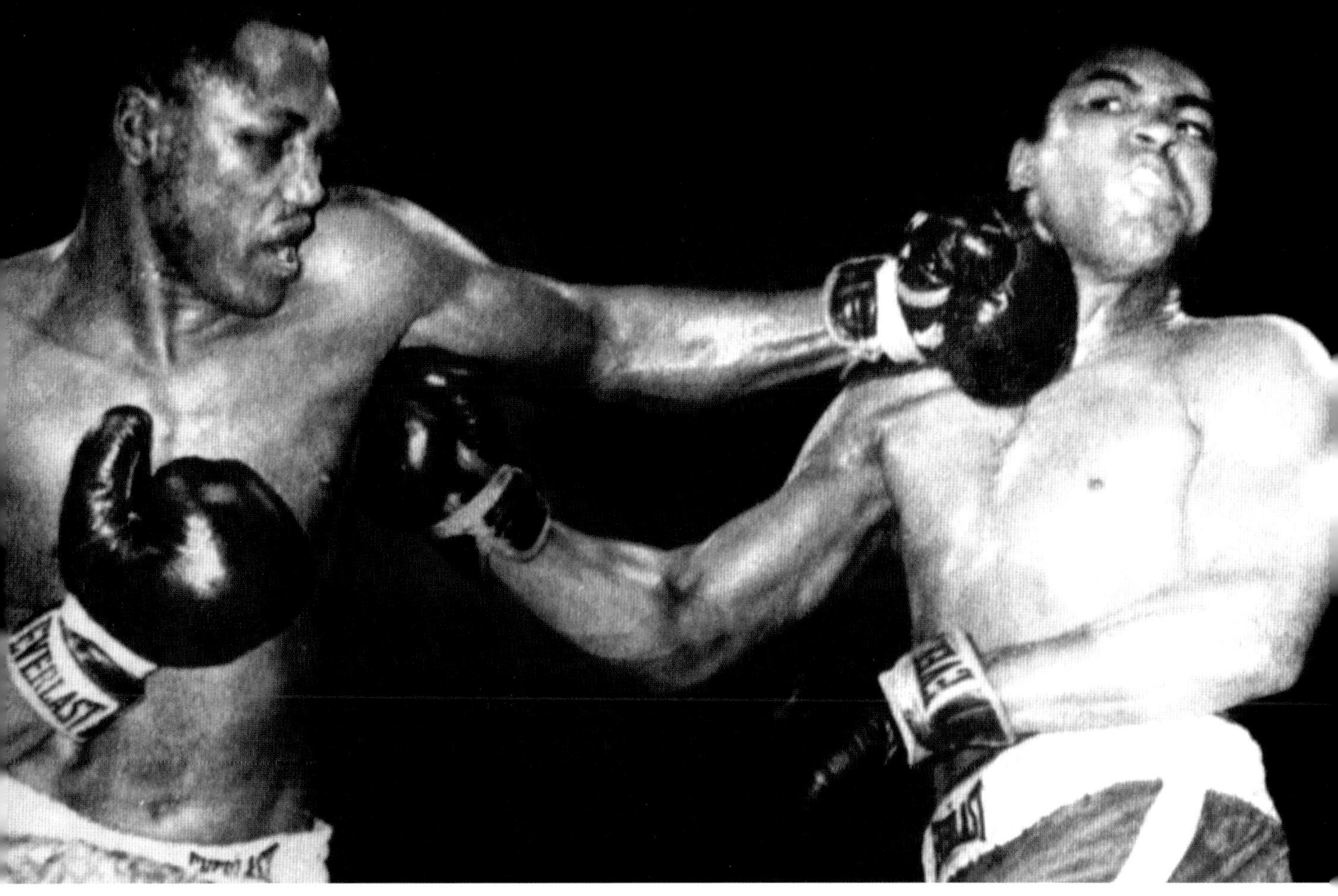

Ali and Joe Frazier. March 8, 1971, New York.

Philadelphia heavyweight named Joe Frazier. Once back from his exile, Ali mocked Frazier without mercy. He resurrected boxing's oldest gimmick – a battle of the races, portraying Frazier, a Black man born in the South, as the white man's champion. It was ludicrous and divisive, but Ali was relentless.

The stage was set for one of the biggest boxing events of all time, a star-crossed collision between two unbeaten young heavyweights, each with a legitimate claim on the championship. It was billed as "The Fight of the Century," and while that phrase was worn out after decades of use, there was no doubting that Ali–Frazier transcended sports. It was, reported *The New York Times*, "the most hysterically ballyhooed promotion of all time," deeming the $5 million split by the fighters as "obscene." Meanwhile, the $1,352,961 paid by 20,455 spectators smashed the record for an indoor

Frazier storms in on Ali during their history-making first bout. New York, 1971.

Sports had entered a new era of high finance. Ali's big mouth meant big money.

live gate, nearly doubling the previous top amount. Sports had entered a new era of high finance. Ali's big mouth meant big money.

At Madison Square Garden on March 8, 1971, Ali and Frazier fought 15 bitter, brutal rounds. This was Ali's chance to reclaim what had been taken from him. Moreover, as the country had grown increasingly opposed to the war, he'd become less of a pariah. Many rooted for Ali to win, especially young people who saw him as an important figure. But the unanimous decision went to Frazier. The bout's climax came in the final round when one of Frazier's sweeping left hooks knocked Ali to the canvas for a count of four. As Ali rose and finished the round, his legion of admirers saw the very character of the man they'd backed, beaten, perhaps, but with an unbreakable spirit.

In June of 1971, the U.S. Supreme Court acquitted Ali of draft evasion. Now free to resume his career unencumbered, he spent the next two years fighting around the world, from Ireland to Japan to Germany. He showed occasional flashes of his past brilliance, but he seemed bored, listless. Training had become distasteful to him. Bursitis in his knuckles made it difficult for Ali to punch with full force. There was also a growing band of female admirers, for whom Ali always made time. Still, he won 10 fights in a row. Calling himself, "The People's Champion," he appeared regularly on the most popular television shows, bantering with hosts on various topics. The spotlight was his again and he relished it.

Ali finally stumbled in early 1973. He lost a 12-round split decision to Ken Norton in San Diego, suffering a broken jaw in the process. Ali had taken Norton lightly, but he avenged the loss six months later, also by split decision. With Norton out of the way, Ali pressed on. By then, however, the heavyweight scene had been upended.

An audience in Kingston, Jamaica, had been shocked in January of 1973 when George Foreman annihilated Frazier in two rounds. Adding to his dossier, Foreman did the same to Norton. Two fighters who had been tough for Ali were nothing for the powerful new champion. He'd squashed them like flies.

As Foreman stood over the heavyweight class like a leviathan, Ali fought Frazier again in January of 1974. Their rivalry hadn't cooled since their first bout, but this time Ali boxed smartly and won a 12-round decision. The path was now cleared for Ali to meet Foreman for the title.

Billed as "The Rumble in the Jungle," the bout took place in Kinshasa, Zaire, on October 31, 1974. While in the land of his ancestors, Ali seemed to harness spiritual energies out of the air. He mingled with locals, and entertained journalists with vivid descriptions of Foreman's impending downfall. Ali's monologues had the effect of incantations. He was turning the traditional prefight buildup into a kind of sorcery.

The 62,000 in attendance saw an unusual fight. Most had expected Ali to use movement to avoid Foreman's heavy punches, but by round two he was leaning on the ropes with his gloves over his face, inviting Foreman to punch away at him. Ali teased Foreman throughout the fight: “Is that all you got? Are you getting tired?” Ali called his odd strategy “The rope-a-dope.” By the fifth round Foreman was arm weary. Ali was firing back.

In the eighth, Ali landed a combination of punches that sent Foreman spinning to the canvas like a helicopter crashing into the sea. Foreman rose, but referee Zach Clayton saw his wobbly condition and waved the fight over. Foreman offered many excuses for his loss, everything from a witch doctor casting a spell on him, to his water being poisoned, to the canvas being too soft. But nothing he said mattered. Ali was champion again.

By now Ali’s celebrity was beyond that of any fighter, athlete, movie star, or politician. He had grandiose aspirations to match. “I had to prove you could be a new kind of Black man,” he said. “I had to show that to the world.”

Ali talked about feeding the hungry and setting up hospitals in poor communities. Mostly, he wanted to inspire people. He once explained to an interviewer his mindset before a fight: “I’m asking God, Allah, to make me strong. Not for me. Don’t give me no money. Don’t give me the fame. I want to win so I can come home and speak for the brother who’s living in rat-infested houses, sleeping on concrete in the ghetto. They can’t go on television and speak. So God, I’m your tool, I’m your servant, let me get this man tonight and go out blasting!”

Approximately one year after beating Foreman, Ali faced Frazier for the third time. The extraordinary “Thrilla in Manila” brought the two rivals together for their final showdown. In the intense Philippine heat, they pounded each other. Ali recalled the punishment he took in that fight as, “the nearest thing to death.” The contest ended when a weary Frazier followed the advice of his corner and didn’t answer the bell for the 15th round. “He’s the greatest next to me,” Ali said after the bout.

The 1976–77 period after Manila was a mixed bag for Ali. His stardom had reached the stratosphere, but the press grew cynical about him. The passionate Black activist of the 1960s was now seen as a huckster

A prime Ali smashes Brian London in a heavyweight title bout. London, 1966.

cashing in on his past. He pitched cheap products on TV, anything from roach spray to deodorant. He even appeared as himself in an autobiographical film called, fittingly, *The Greatest.* DC Comics released a special issue of *Superman* where Ali helped save the world. This was a good metaphor for what he'd become – a cartoon character.

In the ring, he looked old and tired. Challengers he would've once beaten with ease were now pushing Ali to the limit of his abilities. It was an embarrassing night in 1978 when Leon Spinks, fresh from the Olympics but with little pro experience, outhustled Ali to win a unanimous 15-round decision and the championship.

Ashamed by the loss, Ali prepared for one more battle, meeting Spinks for a rematch at the New Orleans Superdome. A crowd of 70,000 paid an astonishing $6 million to witness Ali's probable swansong, setting a record for a live boxing gate at the time. Along with a national television audience, they watched Ali, by now a faded ring general, outfox his younger opponent and win a unanimous decision. The victory gave him the heavyweight championship for an unprecedented third time.

Ali retired in 1979, but he couldn't resist the spotlight. Ali's larger-than-life career ended with humiliating losses to Larry Holmes and Trevor Berbick.

Of greater concern was Ali's health. Though only 40, his slurred speech and hand tremors were that of a much older man. By the mid-1980s he'd been diagnosed with

Ali tags Frazier in their third and final bout, the 1975 "Thrilla in Manila."

Parkinson's Syndrome. It seemed like the cruelest of jokes. The swiftest and most beautiful fighter of all was shutting down. To his confidants Ali would say the affliction was given to him by Allah because he hadn't been a good Muslim. He'd lusted after money, fame, and women. Now, he felt, Allah was testing him.

Most believed boxing had caused his condition, but others felt Ali was genetically predisposed to it. Quack doctors came forth with cures and theories. Fortunately, Ali had married for the fourth time by now and his wife, Lonnie, helped keep the crackpots at bay.

In the meantime, Ali traveled the world in support of various humanitarian causes. He maintained a flair for the dramatic, such as the night in 1996 when, with trembling hands, Ali lit the ceremonial torch to begin the Olympic Games in Atlanta. It was an unforgettable moment. At home, he spent much of his time in prayer and entertained visitors with store-bought magic tricks.

He also made money by appearing at major fights, his presence giving fans a moment to chant "Ali! Ali! Ali!" There was also the passing of the Muhammad Ali Boxing Reform Act in 2000, legislation to improve the safety and welfare of professional boxers and to confirm that promoters were honest about financial dealings. Yet Ali no longer cared about boxing, nor his position in it. "It wasn't important at all," he said. "Boxing was just meant as a way to introduce me to the world."

After the 2001 terrorist attacks on America, Ali released a statement defending Islam as "a religion of peace." There's no telling what Ali's statement meant at a time when hostility toward Muslims was high. But this was his new persona, the spiritual man spreading the word of love.

Ali's legacy wasn't perfect. In retrospect, his mocking of Frazier seemed cruel and unnecessary. For all his worldliness, Ali appeared oblivious to the harm he'd done by using race talk to downgrade opponents. Also, sordid details from his past began to surface. Ex-wives and associates offered unpleasant details of his indiscretions, while

Ali embraces President George W. Bush at the White House after being presented with the Presidential Medal of Freedom in 2005.

biographers depicted him as a cash-hungry rube easily manipulated by promoters and Black Muslim leaders.

Yet these new revelations bounced off the shatterproof Ali image. The public wanted to remember Ali only as a lovable figure from the past, a man who had bravely battled the government and now battled a debilitating illness. As Budd Schulberg wrote of him, "The prickly Black Muslim of 1965, rejected by most of white America as the threatening symbol of Black Power, had somehow morphed into the Black Mother Teresa."

The culture embraced Ali during the 1990s and 2000s. He was the subject of countless books, movies, and documentaries. ESPN Classic aired Ali's old fights on a regular basis; hip-hop artists cited him as an inspiration. As women's boxing grew in popularity, Ali's daughter Laila entered the business. She had some of her dad's charisma, but her brief career often felt like a gimmick.

The various tributes and movie projects kept Ali's image before us like a kind of multimedia hologram. In the meantime, his health declined. He died in 2016 at age 74.

The funeral in Louisville was something one might've seen for a head of state. Ali had become an American hero. There was sadness in the story, in that his boxing prime was taken away by politics, and a disease took away his later years. Yet it appeared his post-boxing life brought him a kind of serenity, and a love from the public that never faded. He once explained this by saying, "I'm more human now."

The big question was whether Ali ever regretted his boxing career and the effect it had on his health. He once addressed this for Louisville writer, Davis Miller. "A man goes to war," Ali said, "fights for his country, comes back with one leg. He either thinks it was worth it or it wasn't.

"I look at all my world fame, the people I've helped, all the things I've done, spiritual and non-spiritual. I add it all up, and I'd do it all over again."

Muhammad Ali Statistics	
Heavyweight Champion	1964–1967, 1974–1978, 1978–1979
Wins	56
KOs	37
Losses	5
Draws	0
Total bouts	61

Foreman wins the heavyweight championship by scoring a second-round knockout of Joe Frazier. Jamaica, 1973.

GEORGE FOREMAN

Full name:	George Edward Foreman
Nickname:	Big George
Birthdate:	January 10, 1949; died March 21, 2025
Place of birth:	Marshall, Texas

From a sneering bully to a jolly folk hero, George Foreman stunned the boxing world with the greatest comeback of all time.

The unique thing about the young George Foreman was that his hitting power came without using the traditional fighter's technique. He didn't appear to need proper leverage, or even accuracy. He'd simply march from his corner at the opening bell, his arms out like a man groping through a blackout, gloves open like enormous cat paws. From this peculiar stance, Foreman could somehow launch devastating punches that erupted like deep-sea depth charges.

True, some smart old trainers, including Archie Moore, tutored Foreman in the finer points of the ring. Yet when his instincts took over, Foreman was most comfortable swinging at opponents like a man wielding a hammer in each hand, confident that no human could stand up to him.

His confidence was well earned. After the briefest amateur career, he'd won a gold medal at the 1968 Olympics in Mexico. Then, as a professional, he'd knocked out 34 of his first 37 opponents.

Still, he was a 3–1 underdog when he faced heavyweight champion Joe Frazier in Kingston, Jamaica, on January 22, 1973. Foreman was overwhelming,

Foreman blew away Jose Roman in one round. Tokyo, Japan, 1973.

knocking Frazier down three times in the first round, and thrice more in the second. At times Frazier seemed airborne, lifted off the canvas by Foreman's punches. At 1:35 of round two, referee Arthur Mercante called a merciful halt to the action.

Shockwaves of disbelief went through movie theaters and arenas across America, all wired for closed-circuit viewings of the bout. The quick massacre was akin to watching a beloved family pet chewed up by a large, seemingly clumsy predator.

Yet the new heavyweight boss had a magnificent story to share.

Foreman was born January 10, 1949, in Marshall, Texas. Growing up in Houston's dangerous Fifth Ward neighborhood, he was a teenage hoodlum going nowhere when he joined the Job Corp, an organization that worked with disadvantaged youths. He took up boxing and earned a spot on the 1968 U.S. Olympic team. He advanced to the finals in Mexico, scoring a second-round stoppage of

During the ceremony when he received his gold medal, Foreman produced a small American flag and waved it proudly.

the vastly more experienced Jonas Čepulis of the Soviet Union. During the ceremony when he received his gold medal, Foreman produced a small American flag and waved it proudly. This was in contrast to the times, when many Black athletes were denouncing the country. Foreman was different. He loved America.

Now that he was champion, Foreman hoped to spread a positive message to the nation's youth, though the championship itself wasn't going to his head.

"The title is borrowed from the people and must be given back," Foreman said. "I plan to take advantage of it while I can, treat everybody good, and when it's time to give it up, I'll do so smiling."

Foreman's first title defense brought him to Japan where he demolished José Roman in less than a round. Then it was off to Venezuela where he destroyed the highly touted Ken Norton in the second round.

Despite his success, Foreman was unhappy. He wasn't making the sort of money he thought was his due. He was also perplexed by the public's cold reaction to him. Though Foreman was the champion, the country and the media seemed far more interested in Muhammad Ali. Moreover, the 6'4", 220-pound Foreman was so strong that he appeared to have an unfair advantage over opponents. As basketball legend Wilt Chamberlain once said, nobody loves Goliath.

By the fall of 1974 when Foreman went to Africa to defend the title against Ali, his surliness was peaking. Ali had nicknamed Foreman "The Mummy," a reference to his slow-moving, ponderous style. Though most journalists were picking Foreman to win, the focus throughout was on Ali. Foreman would admit to being jealous of his charismatic challenger. "I grew meaner by the day," he wrote in his autobiography.

The fight was Foreman's worst nightmare. Ali lay on the ropes and let Foreman swing at him. By the seventh round Foreman was exhausted, undone by Ali's mental games. His vaunted power was useless. To the surprise of the sports world, Ali knocked him down in the eighth. When Foreman rose unsteadily to his feet, he was no longer the champion.

Bitter about losing, Foreman set out to show he was still the most powerful force in boxing. The following April in Toronto's Maple Leaf Gardens, Foreman boxed five opponents on the same afternoon, one after another, for ABC TV's *Wide World of Sports.* The bouts disintegrated into silly melees, with Foreman strutting around the ring sneering and flexing his muscles. It was, wrote the *New York Daily News,* a "disgraceful exhibition."

Foreman followed the Toronto debacle with a few triumphs, including a hellacious brawl with Ron Lyle, won by Foreman in the fifth. Foreman also fought Frazier again, winning in five by a knockout. But in 1977, when he lost a 12-round decision to Jimmy Young in Puerto Rico, Foreman's life changed.

It happened in the stifling hot dressing room of Roberto Clemente Stadium. Foreman claimed to hear the voice of God.

"I could smell death," Foreman said a few years later. "I heard God asking me, 'Why are you afraid to die?' I said I would give my money to charity if God would let me live. But I heard God say, 'I don't want money. I want you.'"

Doctors believed Foreman was merely dehydrated and hallucinating, but he was convinced he'd had a spiritual awakening.

Foreman was soon preaching on the streets of Houston, a Bible in one hand, and a bullhorn in the other. By late 1978 he was an ordained minister. Committed to spreading the word of God, he'd given up boxing at 28 without a second thought. And he seemed happy. He gained weight, and was living modestly with a new wife and several children. In 1981 Foreman told the Associated Press that he was now fighting "devils and false prophets." To make ends meet he sold cleaning supplies.

Foreman struggles to rise in his loss to Muhammad Ali. Zaire, 1974.

The former champion founded a church north of Houston, what one reporter described as "a squat, cinderblock structure that sits among decaying houses and rusting cars like the vestige of a dream." The Church of the Lord Jesus Christ was a bare bones ministry. A handful of old ladies shook tambourines and sang hymns, waiting for their portly preacher to read from the Bible. On some nights Reverend Foreman had less than 10 parishioners. This, it appeared, was how the George Foreman story would end. It wasn't the worst way for a fighter to end up. He had peace of mind. But Foreman's life changed again in 1986.

Foreman's plan was to build a youth center in Houston. The best way to raise money, he decided, was to fight again. The problem was that he was pushing 40 and weighed more than 300 pounds. He trained in secret, lost weight, and went about convincing the boxing authorities that he was not at risk. When a lawyer representing the California attorney general's office asked why he wanted to fight again, Foreman said, "Life,

A different George Foreman emerged in the 1980s.

liberty, and the pursuit of happiness." That seemed to be a good enough answer. He was licensed to fight.

The comeback began with Foreman against a collection of lesser-known fighters in some far-flung locations, including Springfield, Missouri, and Anchorage, Alaska. There was a low-budget feel to Foreman's return, as if he were a washed-up entertainer performing at county fairs. Journalists filled their columns with jokes about Foreman's weight. Rather than be offended, he joked right back, saying he trained on nothing but cheeseburgers. When they mocked the quality of his opponents, Foreman laughed along. "Reporters say I only fight guys on a respirator," he said. "I tell them that's not true. They have to be eight days off a respirator."

Boxing fans, however, were intrigued by the return of George Foreman. They bought tickets to the events and cheered as he jogged to the ring in his frayed red robe, a living, breathing piece of boxing history. Being away for 10 years had somehow endeared him to the public. His menacing glower was gone, replaced by a jolly personality.

His style was different, too. His punches were shorter, crisper. He developed a punishing straight left jab, and borrowed the old-style "cross-armed defense" used by Archie Moore. The 40-year-old Foreman was carrying an additional 30 pounds from his prime days but was calmer and more disciplined than he'd been 15 years earlier.

The first act of his comeback saw him defeat 19 of 20 opponents by KO or TKO. Sometimes he looked clumsy, and his opponents were questionable, but Foreman was selling himself better than any promoter might've done. The fact that he'd named all of his sons "George" endeared him to the public even more.

"I want to show the world turning 40 isn't a death sentence," he said. "You can get better with age."

There was talk that Foreman might fight the notorious heavyweight champion, Mike Tyson, but that idea was scuttled when Tyson lost to James "Buster" Douglas in Tokyo. Douglas, in turn, lost the championship to Evander Holyfield, a former cruiserweight champion and 1984 Olympian.

Though Holyfield was a fine fighter, he needed a big-name opponent to generate interest. With his management not wanting to work with Tyson's promoter, Don King, the search was on for a bankable star to help Holyfield

"I want to show the world turning 40 isn't a death sentence. You can get better with age."
– George Foreman

create an audience. At the time, the best candidate was Foreman.

Foreman challenged Holyfield for the championship in Atlantic City on April 19, 1991. It was a highly anticipated contest with a record setting pay-per-view audience reported to reach one and a half million homes. Granted, there were still many journalists and boxing people who called Foreman a phony who had clowned his way to an astonishing $13 million payday. Yet he was clearly the sentimental favorite. Foreman had charmed America, and many believed he had the so-called "puncher's chance." After 12 rounds, though, it was Holyfield who won by unanimous decision.

Holyfield later admitted that Foreman had hurt him more than once, and at one point in the fight he feared Foreman had knocked out all his teeth. Still, Holyfield was a determined 28-year-old, and superior to the opponents Foreman had faced during his comeback. But if Holyfield won on the scorecards, it was Foreman who won the public's heart. "If Big George never fights again," wrote Budd Schulberg, "he's given us exactly what we need in these days of cynicism when the underclass, the lower class, and even troubled members of the middle class are groping to find a way."

The punchin' preacher had become part of the pop culture. His lovable personality and big presence led to Foreman becoming an effective TV endorser, a friendly face hawking everything from Doritos tortilla chips to Meineke Mufflers. He'd also landed a cushy job as a ringside commentator for HBO, and even starred in a short-lived ABC TV series called *George*.

He could've rested on his newfound celebrity, but Foreman still hoped to win the heavyweight championship. By 1993, however, when he lost a dull decision to Tommy Morrison for the recently established – and lightly regarded – WBO title belt, it appeared the 44-year-old media star was on the way out.

And then he got a break.

In April 1994 Holyfield lost the World Boxing Association (WBA) and International Boxing Fedeation (IBF) titles to a somber young heavyweight named Michael Moorer. Similar to Holyfield a few years earlier, Moorer needed a popular opponent to create interest at the box office. Foreman was a possibility. Now 45, Foreman was viewed as an easy but marketable challenger, a way for Moorer to make some money without much risk.

On November 5, 1994, Foreman came into the fight as a 5–2 underdog. He'd had a dream that he'd knocked Moorer out and was confident he could do it, but he knew it was his last hurrah. The Las Vegas crowd at the MGM Grand Garden Arena cheered as Foreman trotted down the aisle to the ring, the house sound system blaring a recording of Sam Cooke singing "If I Had A Hammer." Symbolically, Foreman wore the same red trunks he'd worn in Africa on the night he lost to Ali, which happened to be almost 20 years to the day earlier. He'd even invited Angelo Dundee, Ali's trainer, to work in his corner during the fight.

Foreman was upbeat but he had a difficult time with Moorer. For nine rounds the younger man offered a cautious, superbly controlled attack, spearing Foreman with his right jab. Foreman's left eye swelled shut. He appeared to be losing every round. But he was laying a trap.

In the 10th, when it seemed Foreman was hopelessly behind on points, he threw a soft jab that caused Moorer to tilt his head to the left. Just then, with a marksman's aim, Foreman shot a quick right to the younger man's chin. Down went Moorer. With glazed eyes, Moorer remained on his back staring up at the arena lights as the referee counted him out. More than one journalist noted that Foreman had thrown a punch 20 years in the making. Foreman might've agreed. "I just got caught," Moorer said. "It's part of boxing."

When it was clear that Foreman had won by knockout, he kneeled in a corner of the ring and gave a quick thanks to God. After the bout, as he addressed the doubters from press row, Foreman recited lyrics from "Over The Rainbow." "Dreams come true," he said. "Look at me tonight."

He had pulled off the greatest comeback in sports history. The title he had once borrowed was his again.

At 45, Foreman was the oldest man to ever win a boxing title. He remains the oldest to win the heavyweight title.

He'd also taken care of something that had bothered him for a long

Foreman hams it up with Archie Moore, who served briefly as Foreman's trainer.

Foreman earned millions selling products, particularly the George Foreman Grill.

time. "I exorcised the ghost (of Ali) once and forever," he said.

Foreman's second reign as champion reminded one of the old adage "getting there is half the fun." His age began to show, and he was stripped of title recognition for not fighting top contenders. His final bout was in 1997 against Shannon Briggs, a hulking 25-year-old. Foreman gave the young man a boxing lesson and rocked him several times, but somehow the judges scored the fight for Briggs. Foreman retired immediately after the bout, saying he was tired of chasing younger men around the ring. "I'm walking away," he said. "I've had a wonderful career." He was weeks away from his 49th birthday.

His final record was 76-5 with 68 knockouts. He was *The Ring's* Fighter of the Year in 1973 and 1976, and was given the same accolade from the Boxing Writers of America in 1973 and 1994. Three times he took part in bouts named Fight of the Year by *The Ring* magazine – his first bout with Frazier, his loss to Ali, and his classic 1976 bout with Lyle. In 1999, he signed an incredible $138 million deal with Salton Inc. to promote The George Foreman Grill. A 2011 *Business Week* article estimated that Foreman had earned $240 million as a product pitchman. What began as a way to raise money for a youth center had evolved into a mammoth empire.

Foreman's death in 2025 was greeted with heartfelt tributes from around the world. It appeared the love and fame he'd craved early in his career was finally his in the end, more than he ever could've imagined back in the 1970s.

Foreman endured his share of problems in life, but he should be considered one of the few fighters to leave boxing and live happily ever after. He not only proved that dreams could come true, but also that a man could reinvent himself. He also showed that it's never too late to go on a grand adventure. For that, we should be in his debt for all time.

George Foreman Statistics	
Heavyweight Champion	1973–1974
WBA, IBF Heavyweight Champion	1994–1995
Wins	76
KOs	68
Losses	5
Draws	0
Total bouts	81

Leonard brought a 1980s sheen to boxing. He was part boxer, part business tycoon.

Sugar Ray Leonard

Full name:	Ray Charles Leonard
Nickname:	Sugar Ray
Birthdate:	May 17, 1956
Place of birth:	Wilmington, North Carolina

With his dazzling style in the ring and his boyish charisma, Ray Leonard introduced America to a new kind of fighter.

Some felt he wasn't made for boxing so much as he was made for television. Yet there was no doubting that Sugar Ray Leonard arrived just in time.

Muhammad Ali was in the twilight of his career, and the brokers of the business saw no one to replace him as the face of boxing. But just as the Ali circus was pulling up stakes, Leonard appeared. A welterweight with quick hands and a bright smile, Leonard was creating a buzz like no one since Ali. Yet despite his abundance of star quality, Leonard had his share of skeptics. On the night he challenged welterweight champion Wilfred Benitez, many still doubted him.

With Leonard earning one million dollars and Benitez guaranteed a shade more, it was to be the richest non-heavyweight bout up to that time. The fight pulled 4,600 spectators to Caesars Palace in Las Vegas, lured there like prospectors to the Klondike. Leonard was the draw. For a rare time in history it appeared that the sport's biggest name did his work well below the heavyweight class. Airing on ABC TV, Leonard–Benitez was the first fight below light heavyweight to headline a prime-time boxing telecast on a

In the fourth defense of his WBC welterweight title, Leonard destroyed Davey Boy Green at 2:27 of round four. Landover, Maryland, 1980.

major network. "Once in a great while a fighter comes along who changes all the numbers," said promoter Bob Arum. Indeed, Leonard had already earned a fortune without even fighting for a championship.

It was Friday night, November 30, 1979, and Las Vegas was hosting not just a big night of boxing, but also the start of a new era. The 1970s were ending, and with the decade closing so went the heartaches of Vietnam and the anger of the Nixon years. The glitz and lowbrow fun of the 1980s were ahead. Though Leonard had won a gold medal at the 1976 Montreal Olympics, he was truly an athlete of the 1980s, reflecting the essence of those years. He was a new kind of fighter, the first boxer-mogul, iridescent with business savvy as well as ring savvy. When he appeared in a television commercial for 7UP, it seemed like a new dawn for boxing. Ali had looked silly in commercials. Leonard was a natural.

He'd landed in Las Vegas like a visiting prince. He posed for pictures with Cher and other celebrities, and spoke to the press about his need to be special. He was not a typical boxer. He was smooth, articulate. Angelo Dundee, who'd spent years as Ali's trainer and now worked with Leonard, was asked by *The New York Times* to compare the two. "I can't compare him to Ali at 23," Dundee said. "Ali was too intricate, too many interests. This kid is home cookin'." Cus D'Amato, the veteran boxing trainer still a few years from unleashing Mike Tyson on the public, proclaimed Leonard "the best finisher since Joe Louis." If boxing fans were a political party, Leonard was their brave new hope for the future.

Because of his refined manners and the fact that he sometimes wore a yachting cap, some dismissed Leonard as something less than a real fighter. He'd never toiled in anonymity – his pro debut was

If boxing fans were a political party, Leonard was their brave new hope for the future.

nationally televised (along with the other gold medalists from 1976) and he'd earned $40,000, unheard of for a pro's first fight. Some were appalled that this upstart called himself "Sugar Ray." There could only be one Sugar Ray, and it was Robinson. Yet the doubters were wrong for thinking Leonard was merely a media creation. He was a fighter down to his core. Still, he was a mystery. "Leonard," said Benitez's manager Jim Jacobs, "is like a beautiful woman. You never know what she is concealing. We'll know after this fight what Leonard may be hiding."

The tension was unbearable from the opening bell. Leonard and Benitez moved cautiously, circling each other like swordsmen. Leonard knocked the champion down in the second round, but by the fifth Benitez was in charge. Benitez was a young genius, younger even than Leonard, with reflexes that had earned him the nickname "El Radar." His jabs turned Leonard's lips puffy.

The momentum kept shifting during the next few rounds, neither man gaining an edge for long, though Leonard hurt Benitez in the ninth, and punched his mouthpiece loose in the 11th, a heated round where Leonard pinned Benitez on the ropes and landed several hard punches. Still, Benitez fought Leonard evenly in rounds 12, 13, and 14. As the climactic 15th began, Dundee told Leonard to close the show in a big way. "Go out there," Dundee said, "and fight like an animal." As he'd do many times in the coming years, Leonard readied himself for an electrifying finish.

For most of the round they stood head-to-head and ripped at each other. Then, with only 30 seconds left, Leonard's left hook got through to Benitez's chin. Benitez wavered and fell. When Benitez rose, referee Carlos Padilla waved the fight on. Leonard rushed in throwing a frenzy of punches until Padilla stepped in and spared Benitez from more punishment.

Leonard skipped his victory celebration and, after getting an x-ray on his throbbing right hand, returned to his suite at Caesars. He spent an hour soaking in a tub, thinking about his future. His reflection in the bathroom mirror was haunting. His face was battered.

Leonard was only 23, but he thought about retiring. He'd never intended to turn pro in the first place. He had only done so to help pay his ill father's medical bills, and to support his new marriage and child. Now he was the welterweight champion.

It was in this moment of pain and uncertainty that the Ray Leonard era began, a stretch of roughly seven years where this fresh-faced kid from Palmer Park, Maryland, would be boxing's biggest attraction.

Belying Leonard's smile and easy manner was a family background of considerable grit, including an older brother who had boxed professionally. Still, it wasn't the lean years in Palmer Park that made headlines. Most of the stories on Leonard focused on his earning potential.

Leonard and his then wife, Juanita, with President Ronald Reagan at the White House. 1981.

With shrewd attorney Mike Trainer as his adviser, Leonard controlled his career like the CEO of a Wall Street firm. Like no fighter had ever done, Leonard dictated how his career took shape. In only a few years he'd earned far more money than Ali, Joe Louis, and Robinson combined. He seemed destined to dominate both boxing and Madison Avenue.

Within a year of winning the World Boxing Council (WBC) welterweight title, Leonard faced Panama's Roberto Durán in June of 1980. With Durán playing the bearded villain to Leonard's squeaky-clean hero, it was the sort of super promotion not seen since the first Ali–Frazier bout in 1971. Fittingly, the contest was held in Montreal, approximately

After a multi-year layoff, Leonard won a 12-round split decision over Marvelous Marvin Hagler. Paradise, Nevada, 1987.

four years after Leonard's Olympic triumph in that city. Though Leonard impressed the critics with his willingness to slug it out, Durán won by unanimous decision.

In the rematch, held five months later in New Orleans, Leonard decided to box rather than brawl. As Leonard danced, teased, and threw bolo punches, Durán grew so frustrated that he quit in the eighth round. When asked if he wanted to continue, an exasperated Durán inadvertently added a new phrase to the boxing lexicon: "No mas!"

Thirty thousand attended Leonard's next outing, a ninth-round stoppage of Ugandan southpaw Ayub Kalule at the Houston Astrodome for the WBA junior middleweight title. Fighting on the undercard was a man who would loom large in Leonard's life, a terror from Detroit named Thomas "Hit Man" Hearns.

In September of 1981 Leonard returned to Caesars Palace to fight Hearns, a tall, fierce welterweight who was regarded as the monster of the division. At the time, Leonard–Hearns was the greatest moneymaking event in sports history. Championships were being splintered among rival sanctioning bodies, and a showdown between the WBA titleholder (Hearns) and the WBC titlist (Leonard) was tantalizing. Advances in pay-tv technology would allow more people to view the fight than ever before, as it was beamed via satellite to 300 U.S. cities and 55 countries, all anxious to see Leonard, the all-American boy, against Hearns, the destroyer. And despite what the *New York Daily News* called its "seemingly cosmic magnitude," the fight lived up to expectations.

Before approximately 25,000 people crowded into a temporary outdoor stadium, and an estimated two million watching on closed-circuit and pay-tv, with heat from the ring lights causing the temperature to reach 110 degrees Fahrenheit, Leonard and Hearns put on an intense fight. Behind on points and with his left eye slammed shut by Hearns's jab, Leonard scored a stirring TKO victory in round 14. Leonard, wrote *Newsday,* was "determined to leave a mark as one of the great fighters of our time. Last night he took a giant step in that direction."

Leonard's career peaked in 1981. He was the undisputed welterweight champion, and the highest paid athlete in the world. *Sports Illustrated* chose him as Sportsman of the Year, and ABC's *Wide World of Sports* named him Athlete of the Year, accolades usually reserved for famous golfers or baseball MVPs. Ali had won both awards in 1974. Now Leonard was in Ali territory.

Leonard's remarkable rise came to an unexpected end in November of 1982. After surgery for a detached retina, the world's most famous fighter announced his retirement from boxing. He attempted a comeback in 1984, stopping journeyman Kevin Howard in nine rounds, but retired again after the fight. "My confidence is not there," Leonard said.

Yet the oft-retiring Leonard returned to face long-reigning middleweight champion Marvelous Marvin Hagler in Las Vegas. The majority of the press and the public thought he was insane for risking his eye and his legacy against the formidable Hagler. Yet on April 6, 1987, Leonard put on a masterful display of boxing and earned a 12-round split decision.

The impressiveness of Leonard's achievement was dampened somewhat by the press's reaction to the verdict. About half of the journalists covering the fight felt that Hagler had been more effective and that two of the three judges had been too easily swayed by Leonard's flashier style, or had leaned toward him for sentimental reasons. Boxing fans were divided as well. Few fights in history have generated as much discussion about the way contests were scored.

Sometimes forgotten in the discussion was that Leonard emerged from a three-year absence and went 12 competitive rounds with an all-time great middleweight. Regardless of how the fight was scored, Leonard had done something astounding. He often said beating Hagler was his proudest moment.

Of course, Leonard had no desire to defend the title he'd taken from Hagler. He promptly retired again, casting the WBC middleweight belt aside.

Leonard wanted complete control, to fight when and whom he wanted, without catering to boxing organizations. He was the ultimate independent operator. Yet Leonard was increasingly viewed as an egotist causing the boxing world to bend to his whims. And it would only get worse.

When he challenged WBC light heavyweight champion Donny Lalonde in 1988, it was stipulated that the 175-pound Lalonde drop down to 168 pounds. This was in order for the newly established WBC super middleweight title to be at stake, along with Lalonde's light heavyweight title. It made no sense for the titles of two weight classes to be contested in one fight. It made even less sense for Lalonde to defend his title while weighing less than his usual fighting weight.

Leonard insisted fighting for the two belts made the fight more of an event.

By claiming two belts, Leonard would be the first fighter to win titles in five weight classes. The distinction sounded impressive but meant little, not with new belts and weight classes being created constantly in the 1980s. Moreover, fighting for two belts went against the rule established in Henry Armstrong's time, one that prohibited fighters from being champion in two weight classes at once. It appeared the WBC didn't know the rule, or didn't care about it. The goal was to placate Leonard, the superstar.

Lalonde was so eager to share a ring with Leonard that he agreed to the unusual double title

Leonard jabs Thomas Hearns during their second bout, a 12-round draw. Paradise, Nevada, 1989.

stipulation and drained himself an additional seven pounds. Though he knocked Leonard down briefly in the fourth, Lalonde was no match for him. Leonard scored a violent knockout in round nine, leaving Lalonde in a heap.

Leonard won his two titles, but immediately gave up the light heavyweight belt. The WBC wouldn't allow him to own two belts at once, which didn't explain why the bout was sanctioned in the first place. Of course, the WBC getting a percentage of Leonard's estimated $15 million purse as a sanctioning fee may have had something to do with it.

In 1989 Leonard battled Hearns again, struggling to earn a draw. Later that year he won a drab, 12-round decision over Durán. But recycling

In retirement, Leonard's gift of the gab made him a natural for the motivational speaking circuit.

old opponents failed to reverse Leonard's decline in popularity.

He still had admirers, but now there was a smattering of boos when Leonard entered the ring. The press that had once praised him for controlling his career now chastised him for exerting too much control, for ensuring everything be on his terms. They viewed his recent opponents as either inexperienced (Lalonde), or past their primes (Hagler, Hearns, Durán). Pete Dexter of the *Sacramento Bee* wrote that Leonard was merely a conniving opportunist, "lying in the tall grass studying the herd for the sick or the slow, waiting for a free lunch." They'd once looked with awe at Leonard's astronomical paydays; now they called him greedy. He was no longer America's sweetheart.

"Leonard has the image of an aristocrat looking down at people," said Madison Square Garden matchmaker Bobby Goodman. "His act has become very, very snooty. Leonard has lost his charm." Irving Rudd, who worked as Leonard's publicist for several fights, put it succinctly in his memoir. "The fact is," Rudd wrote, "I don't think Leonard is a nice guy. Period."

Leonard brushed off the criticism.

"People don't understand what makes me tick, and that bothers them," he said.

Yet Leonard's perfect world was cracking. Longtime camp members were leaving in disputes over money. He and his wife, Juanita, divorced. They'd been the sport's favorite couple – he'd taped a picture of her and their son inside his boot during the Olympics – and now they were done. Leonard was also released from his longstanding job as a commentator on HBO boxing broadcasts. The network replaced him with the jovial George Foreman.

As if he needed proof that his era was over, 34-year-old Leonard lost a humbling 12-round decision to Terry Norris in 1991. Six years later in 1997 he returned at age 40 to face Héctor Camacho. Humiliated by a fifth-round stoppage, it was the only time Leonard didn't hear the final bell of a fight. Later, he reported that he'd injured his leg

"People don't understand what makes me tick, and that bothers them."
– Sugar Ray Leonard

in training, which angered fans who had spent money to see the bout.

He retired with a record of 36-3-1 with 25 KOs. *The Ring* magazine and the Boxing Writers of America selected Leonard as Fighter of the Year in 1979 and 1981. Leonard–Hearns was *The Ring's* Fight of the Year for 1981, while Leonard–Hagler won that same award in 1987. When the 1980s ended, *The Ring* proclaimed Leonard Fighter of the Decade. Of far greater significance than being the first man to win titles in five weight classes, Leonard was the first fighter to earn $100 million.

He didn't become the boardroom leader that many had foreseen, but Leonard's post-boxing life has included work in television and movies, the motivational speaking circuit, and as a boxing promoter. He's also done outstanding work for the Juvenile Diabetes Foundation. He's a more modest person now, using humor to discuss the fears and insecurities that can plague a fighter.

There was also Leonard's 2011 memoir, *The Big Fight*. With surprising frankness, he chronicled his addiction to cocaine and alcohol, his marital difficulties, his compulsive womanizing, a childhood marred by family violence, and an episode from his teen years where he was molested by a couple of older, unnamed mentors. "The book was therapy," Leonard said. "It was cathartic."

The negativity that dogged Leonard in his late career has long since settled but, strangely, so has some of the old fanfare. It's as if the passage of time has somehow nullified Leonard's enormous impact on the business. There's also a tendency among lazy journalists to bundle Leonard with Hearns, Hagler, and Durán, as if they can only be presented as a quartet. This is a disservice to all four, but especially Leonard. He didn't need the others to be a star. As great as they were, it was Leonard who gripped the general public, not his opponents.

Leonard's fights were small masterpieces, sporting events that bled over into the mainstream. If nothing else, he proved that fighters of the lighter weight classes could carry the business. To say he replaced Ali is wrong, for his effect on the public was never as vast nor as deep, though on the short list of fighters who could be considered boxing saviors, Leonard shined brighter than most. His ego got in the way at times, but as Leonard said during one of his many comebacks, "My ego is what made me who I am."

Sugar Ray Leonard Statistics	
WBC Welterweight Champion	1979–1980, 1980–1981 (Undisputed Welterweight Champion 1981–1982)
WBA Junior Middleweight Champion	1981
WBC Middleweight Champion	1987
WBC Light Heavyweight Champion	1988
WBC Super Middleweight Champion	1988–1990
Wins	36
KOs	25
Losses	3
Draws	1
Total bouts	40

Mike Tyson captured the American public's imagination as few fighters ever had before.

MIKE TYSON

Full name:	Michael Gerard Tyson
Nickname:	Iron Mike, The Baddest Man on the Planet
Birthdate:	June 30, 1966
Place of birth:	Brooklyn, New York

Boxing's youngest heavyweight champion always seemed on a path of self-destruction.

The morning after Mike Tyson defeated Trevor Berbick for the WBC heavyweight title was like the sunrise after a stormy night. It was November 1986 and boxing was resurrecting itself again, this time with the help of an explosive young fighter from New York. At one point Tyson hit Berbick so hard that the defending titleholder fell, got up, and then fell twice more, his equilibrium scattered from the force of Tyson's punch. As Berbick struggled to stand upright, referee Mills Lane stopped the bout at 2:35 of round two. Berbick falling three times from a single punch was unlike anything anyone had ever seen. For that matter, so was Tyson. At 20, Tyson was the youngest man to win the heavyweight title.

"I was coming to destroy him and I did," Tyson said. "I feel I can beat anybody in the world."

Tyson's rise played out like a storybook. A troubled kid from The Tryon School for Boys, Tyson was taken in by an elderly boxing trainer, Cus D'Amato, who filled his head with dreams of fame. Soon, the teenage crook from Brownsville was living in the Catskills with D'Amato, studying old fight films and learning how to intimidate opponents. "You'll reign with the gods," D'Amato told him.

Tyson stopped England's Frank Bruno at 2:55 of round five. Winchester, Nevada, 1989.

The old man died before he could see his protégé bloom, but the riches and fame came as promised. There would also be several years of tumult and scandal.

Armchair psychologists thought D'Amato's death caused the young fighter's derailment. Yet even when D'Amato was alive there were stories of Tyson behaving badly. He had no impulse control, especially around females.

Tyson's upbringing had been ugly. He was from the Brownsville section of Brooklyn, what he called "a gruesome kind of place." Abandoned by his father and raised by a mother who occasionally slept with men for money, Tyson's upbringing would've traumatized anyone. Brownsville was a decaying, neglected area overrun with crime, drugs, and prostitution. He overcame bullying by neighborhood kids and became a bully in his own right. His childhood was soon marked by petty crimes, gang activity, and violence. After several incidents, he ended up at Tryon. He entered the school's boxing program, where an instructor noticed him and contacted D'Amato, anxious to tell him about this gigantic and vicious 13-year-old.

That an elderly mentor plucked him from obscurity gave Tyson's story a Dickensian feel. There was also a Frankensteinish tone to it, as D'Amato seemed bent on creating the perfect fighting machine. D'Amato even used hypnosis to build up Tyson's self-confidence. "Sometimes he didn't even have to talk," Tyson claimed. "I could feel his words coming through my mind telepathically."

Tyson developed a reverence for old-time fighters, which endeared him to the old-time writers. They liked the way he recycled D'Amato's lines about "fire and fear," and the way he talked about hitting his opponents with "bad intentions." Tyson was good copy, even if his best lines were lifted from movies and gangsta rap songs. He may not have had an original thought in his head, but he had a politician's instinct for telling people what they wanted to hear. He raised pigeons, too, showing his gentle side.

He was a dynamo in the ring, having mastered the D'Amato "peek-a-boo" style. Short for a heavyweight at 5'11", but thickly built at 220 pounds, Tyson was a perfect blend of power and speed. He was an awesome sight, crouching down, boring into opponents, swiveling his head and torso with machine-like precision, maneuvering until he found the opening and then, with bloodcurdling quickness, landing ferocious uppercuts and hooks. He was the heavyweight the world had been waiting for, a throwback to the knockout punchers of the past.

He came to the ring wearing no robe or socks, the classic gladiator stripped for battle. In a time when fighters haggled over paydays and opponents, the public was immediately intrigued by Tyson's readiness to fight.

"I took it back to its raw form," Tyson once said. "Kill or be killed. The winner gets it all. That's what people want. I gave everybody what they want. And they paid me for it."

“Kill or be killed. The winner gets it all. That’s what people want. I gave everybody what they want. And they paid me for it.”

– Mike Tyson

The stories piled up, like the time in Atlantic City when he punched a hole in the wall of his dressing room before going out to KO Michael Spinks in 91 seconds, or the way he clobbered a former opponent, Mitch Green, in a street fight in the middle of Harlem. All of this helped make Tyson into a sort of legend before his time.

As would be expected for a heavyweight champion from New York, Tyson was given intense mainstream coverage. Then came endorsement deals with Toyota, Kodak, Diet Pepsi, and Nintendo. *The Ring* and the Boxing Writers Association selected Tyson as Fighter of the Year in 1986 and 1988. Yet the awards and commercial spots seemed like trifles against what was being predicted for Tyson. Before he’d had 30 fights it was almost unanimously agreed that he would be the greatest heavyweight of them all.

Still, there was a recklessness about him: a car crash put Tyson in the hospital in 1988; a stormy, eight-month marriage to sitcom star Robin Givens made Tyson a tabloid favorite, particularly when she accused him of abusive behavior, while an alliance with controversial promoter Don King made Tyson appear foolhardy. In a short amount of time the inner circle of people that had helped Tyson since the D’Amato days was gone. Nevertheless, experts believed there was no way greatness could elude this young man.

For a while, that was true. The bout with Spinks set new records for box office and viewership, and established Tyson as the undisputed heavyweight champion. However, the discord in Tyson’s life caught up to him. In February 1990, he went to Tokyo to face a 42–1 underdog, James “Buster” Douglas. In the most surprising boxing upset of all time, a highly motivated Douglas took

In one of the highest grossing bouts in boxing history, Tyson knocked out Michael Spinks at 1:31 of round one. Atlantic City, 1988.

advantage of an unfocused Tyson to score a remarkable 10th round KO.

Tyson's mask of invincibility had been yanked off. Underneath was a confused young man, already addicted to the indulgences of fame, and increasingly surrounded by sycophants and gold-diggers.

Tyson's decline continued in 1992 when he was sent to an Indiana prison on a rape conviction. To this day Tyson denies the charge, but the trial portrayed him as an out-of-control deviant.

In prison he embraced the Muslim faith, read the works of Hemingway and Voltaire and, as he claimed later, had sex with female guards and even his drug counselor.

Upon his release in 1995, he was no longer Tyson the fighter. He was Tyson the spectacle. It was the era of shock and sleaze, where daytime talk shows put the spotlight on vulgar guests, murderers became media stars, and the public generally was more accepting of conduct not previously tolerated. Tyson thrived in this tacky

Tyson defeated Andrew Golota in two rounds, but the result was thrown out when Tyson failed a drug test. Auburn Hills, Michigan, 2000.

culture like a snake in a sewer. (How perfect that his eventual memoir, *Undisputed Truth,* would be co-written by Larry Sloman, who'd co-written books by the personification of bad taste, radio personality Howard Stern.)

Though his intimidating image was still intact, Tyson's time behind bars had eroded his skills. He scored a few quick wins and even regained the WBC and WBA belts, which said more about the heavyweight division's sad state than what remained of his prowess.

Tyson's comeback imploded in November of 1996 when he faced Evander Holyfield in Las Vegas. Holyfield was considered past his prime, but he wore Tyson down and scored an 11th round TKO. After the fight, Tyson shook Holyfield's hand and thanked him.

The rematch in 1997 smashed all records for viewership and reportedly earned more than $100 million in pay-per-view buys. Yet with the biggest audience ever for a boxing event, Tyson hit a new low. He was disqualified in the third round for biting Holyfield's ears. He would claim the bites were in retaliation for Holyfield having butted him, but most saw the incident as Tyson bailing out of a fight he knew he couldn't win.

The next few years were a haze of psychiatric evaluations and progressively strange behavior. Barred from fighting in Nevada, Tyson brought his lunatic act to Michigan, then to England, Scotland, Denmark, any location where curiosity seekers would pay to see his traveling freak show. He struck opponents while they were down; he failed drug tests; he hit a referee. A road rage incident sent Tyson to prison again in 1999.

During this portion of his career, Tyson gave several unhinged interviews. He ranted about his tormented past, compared himself to Alexander the Great, and titillated the public with glimpses into his damaged psyche. He portrayed himself as a remorseless monster, the product of a sick society. In 2001, he told reporters, "I'm on the Zoloft to keep me from killing y'all."

Much of Tyson's raving sounded contrived, but it kept his name in the news. He seemed especially unbalanced when discussing reigning champion Lennox Lewis. "I want his heart," Tyson said. "I want to eat his children." At the press conference to announce the 2002 Lewis–Tyson bout, a riot broke out on the dais. During the scuffle, Tyson bit Lewis on the leg.

Deeply in debt and not in his right mind, Tyson had become the train wreck from which the public couldn't look away. "I see Tyson as a tragic figure," wrote Jack Newfield. "He has no job skill other than hitting people."

When they eventually met at the Pyramid in Memphis, Tennessee, on June 8, 2002, Lewis dominated Tyson and knocked him out at 2:25 of round eight.

Tyson was done. Sure, there was more to come: the Māori tattoo on his face, the lions and tigers he kept as

In time, people overlooked his repulsive side and remembered him instead as entertaining and exciting.

pets, his ever-growing debt, a Nevada mansion full of life-sized statues of his favorite pillagers: Genghis Khan, Hannibal, etc. There was a divorce from his second wife, more outbursts, more ranting, epic revels in Las Vegas with his posse of yes-men. But as a fighter he was done.

The Tyson story fizzled out at the MCI Center in Washington DC in 2005. Against a tall, undistinguished Irish journeyman named Kevin McBride, Tyson showed nothing. He didn't come out for the seventh round. "I don't think I have it anymore," Tyson said. There were boos as Tyson left the ring. The fighter who had come to embody America's obsessions with race, class, machismo, violence and fame was, in the end, just another shopworn pug hearing jeers.

The loss to McBride left Tyson's record at 50-6, with 44 knockouts and a couple of no-contests. As an attraction, Tyson had no equals in his day. The Holyfield rematch and the bout with Lewis set new records for pay-per-view buys, with each drawing nearly two million paid viewers. Tyson–Holyfield II was the first boxing match to earn over $100 million in revenue. Tyson's first reign as champion was just a bit more than three years, a good but not great length of time. His second title run, post-prison, lasted seven months.

At the time of his retirement, there was some argument as to where Tyson ranked among the all-time greats. Many considered Tyson the king of squandered potential. He'd disgraced the business and lacked certain traits that are usually required of the great ones. For instance, he never avenged any of his defeats. The great ones did. He didn't. Though most agreed Tyson was devastating in his early days, his critics argued that he looked his best against weak or aging opponents. Against better fighters he was less convincing. Most glaring was Tyson's weakness of character. If he couldn't intimidate you, he struggled. When a fight became difficult, he resorted to fouls.

Tyson looks strong against Danny Williams but was stopped in the fourth round. Kentucky, 2003.

Still, the public missed Tyson when he was gone. In time, people overlooked his repulsive side and remembered him instead as entertaining and exciting. Thanks to America's infatuation with bad boys, he grew into an iconic figure. When he appears in public with Holyfield or Lewis, it is Tyson who gets the grand ovation, not the men who beat him.

Part of this is because Tyson has endured some calamities, including bankruptcy, addictions to drugs and alcohol, and the death of one of his children in a household accident. His supporters see him as a vulnerable man who was wronged

An all-too-common sight from late in Tyson's career.

by the judicial system, promoters, and women. That he blew through more than $400 million is not viewed as an embarrassment, but as proof of his ferocious lifestyle. To his admirers, the Tyson who lost to the likes of Douglas, Holyfield, and Lewis wasn't the real Tyson. They prefer to watch the quick, highlight reel knockouts from early in his career.

Though he credits his third wife, Lakiha Spicer, with helping to keep him stable, Tyson has done a remarkable job of rehabbing his image. After many years depicting himself as a man to be feared, he lampooned his reputation with cameos in comedy films, and lent his voice to a wacky cartoon series called *The Mike Tyson Mysteries.*

He's shown an ex-villain's most endearing quality: a willingness to poke fun at himself.

Tyson's reinvention is on par with George Foreman becoming good-humored, or John L. Sullivan becoming anti-alcohol. Tyson, the scourge, has become contrite and self-aware. He's like the screwed-up old rock star who has survived his crazy life and lived to joke about it. One moment he's recalling the time he nearly beat up Brad Pitt, then he's telling about offering a zookeeper $100,000 because he wanted to fight a silverback gorilla. He's also adept at sharing what he's learned from self-help books and years of therapy. His admirers hang on his every word, as if listening to a sage. Sometimes he weeps.

In *Tyson*, a 2008 documentary by filmmaker James Toback, he was a frank, compelling subject. This was followed by his one-man stage show, *The Undisputed Truth*, directed by Spike Lee and performed on HBO and around the world. Perhaps the irony was lost on Tyson and Lee, but Tyson's soul baring had become an "act," a routine to summon at a moment's notice, like a favorite old dance step. Tyson's 2013 autobiography was 557 pages of harrowing revelations and self-loathing. Though many were impressed by his candor, some felt it was merely a continuation of the madman routine he'd done for years.

He's always been coy about his image. Tyson is often praised for being genuine, but the truth is that his persona has been carefully cultivated since the beginning of his career. He's a master at marketing himself. "Some of it you can believe," Tyson once said of his wildest stories, "and some is bull."

He remains highly visible. A vocal marijuana advocate, he owns a cannabis ranch in Arizona. Between 2019 and 2023 he hosted nearly 200 episodes of a podcast, *Hotboxin' with Mike Tyson*. In 2024 he opened a school in Phoenix for grades six through 12, and often supports charitable causes. He portrays himself now as a humble family man who goes with

Tyson reinvented himself as a storyteller. His one-man show played on stages around the world.

the flow of life, bemused by how things have turned out for him.

"Life is just a circle," he has said. "They're gonna hate me again one day. Then, God willing, they're gonna respect me again one day."

He also appears to have come to terms with his past, telling *GQ* in 2023 that it was all "ordained. It was the way it was supposed to be. The ordeals, the people dying; it's just the way it was supposed to be."

In 2020 Tyson boxed a six-round exhibition with Roy Jones Jr. The glorified sparring session between two men in their 50s pulled in 1,600,000 buys on pay-per-view. In 2024, Tyson fought YouTube personality Jake Paul in a bout shown on Netflix. Fans were disappointed. Tyson looked every bit of his 58 years and lost an eight-round unanimous decision. Still, the reported 108-million global viewers broke all records for streaming sports events. These later-in-life efforts proved that Tyson's appeal, if not his punch, was stronger than ever.

Regardless of whether he lived up to expectations, Tyson's imprint on boxing is indelible. His most impressive victory was not over another opponent, but over the American consciousness. It is there, in our daydreams, that he occupies a seemingly permanent space.

Mike Tyson Statistics	
WBC, WBA, and IBF Heavyweight Champion	1986–1990
WBC, WBA Heavyweight Champion	1997
Wins	50
KOs	44
Losses	7
Draws	0
No-contests	2
Total bouts	59

Honorable Mentions

Had I been allowed a 16th Immortal, many of the following fighters would've fit. But even this second list was troublesome. Great fighters kept coming to mind (Max Baer, Ike Williams, Sonny Liston) but something always prevented their inclusion. Some were great, but only briefly. Some were well-known to boxing fans, but less meaningful to the public. All I can say is that America launched many excellent boxers, and shaving the list down to the Immortals was a challenge. With due respect to those not included, here are my honorable mentions listed by year of birth.

Joe Gans
1874–1910

The first American born Black champion, Gans was both clever and dangerous in the ring. His record of 147-10-16 with 20 no-decision bouts and 101 wins by knockout is among the best in boxing history. His reign as lightweight champion spanned from 1902 to 1908 and included 15 title defenses, a record that stood for nearly a century. Though he was accused more than once of betting on an opponent and then faking a loss, Gans was one of the most revered fighters of his day, known affectionately as "The Old Master." He died of tuberculosis in 1910 at age 35.

James J. Jeffries
1875–1953

This 6'1", 220-pound powerhouse was a grizzly bear of a man known for his incredible strength. His post-retirement comeback loss to Jack Johnson didn't diminish Jeffries' place in the hearts of his admirers.

Jeffries' career was highlighted by two memorable victories over "Sailor Tom" Sharkey, one a 20-round decision in San Francisco in 1898, the other a 25-round decision at the Coney Island Athletic Club in 1899. Jeffries' final record was 19-1-2, with 16 KOs and 2 no-contests. In only 24 outings, he left behind a reputation for fearlessness and determination.

Terry McGovern 1880–1918

A flinty, hotheaded Irish lad fighting out of Brooklyn, NY, McGovern became so popular that young men throughout the city copied his hairstyle. He was John L. Sullivan in miniature, an obstinate and reckless battler who provided thrills in the ring, and inspiration for the Irish American population. Being managed by the Broadway team of Sam Harris and Joe Humphries guaranteed McGovern's career would never be short of ballyhoo. It also led to his appearing in a series of successful stage productions. Few fighters ever combined McGovern's savagery in the ring with such outright showbiz flair, which was double impressive for a fighter rarely weighing more than 122 pounds.

A champion at bantamweight and featherweight, "Terrible Terry" posted a final record of 60-4-3 with 45 knockouts and 12 no-decisions. Mental illness and alcoholism led to McGovern's death at 37, but his devotees praised him long after he was gone. He was certainly America's most beloved fighter since Sullivan, and in an ironic twist, his death came only 22 days after Sullivan's passing.

Stanley Ketchel 1886–1910

Known as "The Michigan Assassin," Ketchel left behind a record of 49-5-3, with four no-decisions, one no-contest, and 46 knockouts. Though only a middleweight, he fought some of the best heavyweights of his era, including Jack Johnson and Sam Langford. His most notable achievement may have been his wild four-bout series with Billy Papke, of which Ketchel won three.

Being murdered at 24 by an itinerant ranch hand in Missouri gave Ketchel's story a tragic, outlaw appeal. Even without his untimely death, there will always be room for his name on any list of great middleweights.

Gene Tunney 1897–1978

If defeating Jack Dempsey for the heavyweight championship was Tunney's greatest moment, it was also a kind of curse. Dempsey was one of the most magnetic sports heroes of the 1920s, and the public never quite forgave Tunney for supplanting him. Deep down, Tunney understood this. After the infamous Chicago rematch when he defeated Dempsey again (and became the first fighter to earn a million-dollar paycheck), Tunney made only one title defense. It was an 11th round stoppage of New Zealand's Tom Heeney at Yankee Stadium on July 26, 1928. It only drew about half the spectators of a Dempsey fight, which showed what ticket buyers thought of the new champion. With no interesting challengers on the horizon, Tunney retired from boxing at age 31.

The press and the public perceived Tunney as too intellectual. But despite his love of Shakespeare, Tunney was a master boxer and a cunning strategist. He retired as champion with a sterling record of 65-1-1, with 48 knockouts and 17 no-decision bouts. He was also highly decorated for his military service during World Wars I and II.

Mickey Walker 1901–1981

"I'll fight a lion if the price is right," Walker once said. No one doubted him. Though no lions appear on his record, Walker fought through a veritable jungle of great fighters. He won the welterweight title from Jack Britton in 1922, and though he failed to win the middleweight title from Harry Greb, he would win the middleweight laurels in 1926 by beating Greb's conqueror, Tiger Flowers.

Dubbed "The Toy Bulldog" for his short stature, Walker didn't let his size prevent him from challenging much bigger men. Walker's final record was 94-19-4, with 60 wins by knockout and 45 no-decision bouts. He later found success as an artist and saw his work exhibited around the world. Sadly, he died penniless in a New Jersey hospital.

Tony Canzoneri 1908–1959

It was unlikely that a kid from Louisiana could become the toast of New York, but that's how life went for Tony Canzoneri. Known as "Canzi," or "Little Paisan," he amassed a record of 137-24-10 with 44 knockouts and 4 no-decision bouts. A champion at featherweight, lightweight, and junior welterweight, he scored victories over the likes of Johnny Dundee, Benny Bass, Jack "Kid" Berg, Kid Chocolate, Billy Petrolle, Baby Arizmendi, Jimmy McLarnin, and Lou Ambers. "Almost every fight Tony Canzoneri engaged in became a memorable one," wrote the *Daily News* at the time of his death in 1959.

Among the high points of Canzoneri's 14-year career was a fight that took place in New York on November 14, 1930. That was the night he knocked out Al Singer in 66 seconds to win the lightweight title. The result was so shocking that some journalists thought it was a fake.

Canzoneri retired from boxing in 1939 but remained a fixture along Broadway. He owned a saloon and became part of a nightclub act with comic Joey Adams.

Barney Ross 1909–1967

Born Dov-Bear Rosofsky, Ross was one of the prominent Jewish fighters of the 1930s. He won championships at lightweight and welterweight, and for a time was recognized as champion of the fledgling junior welterweight class. *The Ring* named him Fighter of the Year in 1934 (an award he shared with Tony Canzoneri) and '35. He retired from boxing with a record of 72-4-3, with two no-decision bouts and 22 wins by knockout.

Ross later served as a marine during WWII, where he earned a Silver Star. After the war he developed an addiction to heroin, which became the subject of his memoir, *No Man Stands Alone*. The book was made into a film with the more lurid title, *Monkey on my Back*.

Ross's boxing career included memorable rivalries with other greats of the day, including Canzoneri, Jimmy McLarnin, and Ceferino Garcia. His final bout was a 15-round loss to Henry Armstrong at the Madison Square Garden Bowl. Among lightweights and welterweights, few could compare to this little gem of a fighter, a man hailed by his fans as "The Pride of the Ghetto."

Ezzard Charles 1921–1975

A fighter with three wins over Archie Moore has to be mentioned in any discussion of boxing Immortals. Add to this his wins over some of the key names of the 1940s, including two over Charley Burley, four over Jimmy Bivins, and five over Joey Maxim. That's quite a resume, and it belongs to "The Cincinnati Cobra," Ezzard Charles.

Using an elegant style mixed with occasional ferocity, Charles was one of the best light heavyweights of all time. In 1949 he earned a 15-round decision over Jersey Joe Walcott to win the NBA heavyweight title vacated by Joe Louis. When Louis returned in 1950, Charles beat him by 15-round decision to earn unanimous recognition as champion. He lost the title to Walcott in 1951, and then failed in two gallant challenges of Rocky Marciano.

He was *The Ring* magazine's Fighter of the Year in 1949 and 1950, one of a handful of names to win the award in consecutive years. His final record was 95-25-1 with 52 KOs, most of the losses coming late in his career. Charles died of ALS in 1975.

Jake LaMotta 1922–2017

It is fitting that his name is permanently etched next to Ray Robinson's. Though Robinson led their six-fight series 5-1, a couple of their bouts were razor close, and the rivalry could've easily been tied at three apiece. Yet there was more to LaMotta than merely being the stone upon which Robinson sharpened himself.

LaMotta's reluctance to cooperate with the gangland influence of the day kept him on the fringes of the business for years. After his retirement he admitted to throwing a fight against Billy Fox in order to secure a title shot against the middleweight champion, Marcel Cerdan, in 1949. His confession helped expose the Mafia's influence on boxing but made him a pariah.

In 1980 Robert DeNiro portrayed LaMotta in *Raging Bull,* a film based on LaMotta's autobiography. The movie spawned a new appreciation for LaMotta, even if some still considered him a lowlife. His record – 83-19-4 with 30 KOs – was achieved against such stars as Laurent Dauthuille, Robert Villemain, and Fritzie Zivic. Known for his ability to take punishment, LaMotta was knocked down only once in 106 fights.

Sandy Saddler 1926–2001

Best known for winning three of four bouts against Willie Pep, Saddler had an amazing career beyond that memorable series. A champion at both featherweight (twice) and junior lightweight, he scored wins over Joe Brown, Paddy DeMarco, Harold Dade, Lauro Salas, Teddy Davis, and the legendary Philippine boxer, Gabriel "Flash" Elorde.

At 5'8" Saddler was tall for a featherweight and thin as a post. A.J. Liebling of *The New Yorker* once described him as "built like a bundle of loosely joined fishing poles." Yet Saddler's slim frame masked some incredible power; he was one of the great punchers of all time. He retired at age 30 after suffering injuries in a car accident. Saddler's overall record was 145-16-2, with 104 knockouts.

Joe Frazier 1944–2011

Emerging from the 1964 Tokyo Olympics with a gold medal and a style that screamed excitement, "Smokin' Joe" Frazier earned unanimous acclaim as heavyweight champion with a fourth-round knockout of Jimmy Ellis in 1970. He was *The Ring* magazine's Fighter of the Year in 1967, 1970, and 1971.

The highlight of Frazier's career was his iconic first bout with Muhammad Ali in 1971. Frazier won by 15-round decision, but the toll on him was devastating. After a hospital stay and a gradual return to boxing, he lost the title in two rounds to George Foreman in 1973. Though he remained a force in the business and took Ali to the edge in their grueling 1975 bout in the Philippines, it appeared Frazier was no longer the destructive slugger he'd once been. Suffering from vision problems and other ailments, he finished his career in 1981.

His record – 32-4-1 with 27 knockouts – was compiled against the best competition of his day. Yet Frazier's place in boxing history was guaranteed the night he defeated Ali with the whole world watching.

Larry Holmes 1949–

His 22 successful defenses of the heavyweight title nearly matched the record of 25 set by Joe Louis, and when he reached his 48th consecutive victory without a loss he was on the verge of matching Rocky Marciano's undefeated record. Larry Holmes missed hitting those milestones, but he deserves a place among the greats.

His record stands at 69-6 with 44 KOs. His most famous bouts were his 15-round decision over Ken Norton to claim the WBC heavyweight title in 1978, his 11th round TKO of the faded Ali in 1980, and his 13th round TKO of Gerry Cooney in 1982, which was one of the most widely viewed heavyweight bouts in history. Holmes was *The Ring's* Fighter of the Year in 1982.

It was Holmes's bad luck to follow Ali's reign, and many dismissed him as a poor copy of "The Greatest." Yet he possessed an outstanding left jab, a punishing right hand, and excellent mobility. He was also known for his durability and toughness. He lost his title to Michael Spinks in 1985, and was unsuccessful in subsequent attempts to regain the championship. Holmes's final bout was at age 52, a 10-round decision over "Butterbean" Esch in 2002.

Marvelous Marvin Hagler 1954–2021

He spent years struggling for recognition, but Hagler emerged in the 1980s as one of the great middleweight champions of all time. A dangerous southpaw who could easily switch to a right-handed stance, he made 12 successful title defenses. His career highlight was his third-round knockout of Thomas Hearns in 1985, a thriller regarded as one of the greatest fights in boxing history, one that will, indeed, be remembered forever.

His final bout was a close, split decision loss to Sugar Ray Leonard in 1987.

Bitter over the result, Hagler retired with a record of 63-3-2 with 52 knockouts. He had been *The Ring's* Fighter of the Year in 1983 and 1985. A poll by *Boxing Illustrated* in 1990 named him Fighter of the Decade. After boxing he lived full-time in Italy where he acted in some movies, and occasionally served as a commentator for boxing broadcasts.

Evander Holyfield 1962–

In only his 12th pro fight, Holyfield won the WBA cruiserweight title in 1986 with a hellacious 15-round split decision over Dwight Qawi. Using weightlifting techniques to add size to his frame, he journeyed into the heavyweight class, winning that division's title with a third-round knockout of Buster Douglas in 1990. There were also thrilling bouts with Michael Dokes, Bert Cooper, George Foreman, and his memorable trilogy with Riddick Bowe.

At age 34 he surprised the boxing world with an 11th round stoppage of Mike Tyson for the WBA heavyweight title. The 1997 rematch saw Tyson disqualified after biting Holyfield's ears.

Holyfield continued on for another 14 years, often at odds with commission authorities concerned about his safety. Allegations of steroid use soiled his reputation somewhat, but Holyfield will be remembered as one of the greats of the post Ali era. He was a three-time *Ring* magazine Fighter of the Year (1987, 1996, 1997) and posted a final record of 44-10-2 with 29 KOs.

Floyd Mayweather Jr. 1977–

When it came to winning fights and making money, Floyd Mayweather Jr. was a master. Unsurpassed at sizing up an opponent's style and nullifying it, Mayweather baffled rivals with old-school defensive techniques passed down by his father, Floyd Sr., and his Uncle Roger, fine fighters in their own right.

On the way to compiling his pristine record of 50-0 with 27 KOs, Mayweather collected 15 title belts in five weight classes and earned *The Ring* magazine's Fighter of the Year award in 1998 and 2007. Meanwhile, his bouts with Oscar De La Hoya, Manny Pacquiao, and MMA star Conor McGregor shattered old totals for pay-per-view buys. Granted, Mayweather needed those marquee opponents to draw such impressive numbers, but he was a shrewd businessman and became the wealthiest boxer in history.

Some will always debate his merits. His fights were often clinical rather than exciting, and in comparison to Ali or Louis he had little impact on the culture. But his clinical style kept him undefeated, and it is doubtful that any fighter could match Ali or Louis as far as cultural impact. It is enough to say that Mayweather's impact was in the world of boxing. His place among America's greats is secure.

Bibliography

Books

Armstrong, Henry, *Gloves, Glory, and God: An Autobiography*, Fleming H. Revell Company, 1956.

Boyd, Herb and Ray Robinson II, *Pound for Pound*, Amistad, 2005.

Brenner, Teddy, with Barney Nagler, *Only the Ring Was Square*, Prentice Hall, Inc. Englewood Cliffs, New Jersey, 1981.

Brunt, Howard, *Facing Ali*, Lyons Press, New York, 2003.

Dempsey, Jack with Barbara Piattelli Dempsey, *Dempsey*, Harper & Row, New York, 1977.

Fleischer, Nat, *50 Years at Ringside*, Fleet Publishing Corporation, New York, 1958.

Fried, Ronald K., *Corner Men: Great Boxing Trainers*, Four Walls Eight Windows, New York, 1991.

Heinz, W.C., *Once They Heard the Cheers*, Doubleday, New York, 1979.

Heller, Peter, *In This Corner...! 42 World Champions Tell Their Stories*, Da Capo Press, New York, 1994.

Izenberg, Jerry, *Once There Were Giants*, Skyhorse Publishing, 2017.

Kahn, Roger, *A Flame of Pure Fire, Jack Dempsey and the Roaring '20s*, Harcourt Inc., New York, 1999.

Klein, Christopher, *Strong Boy, The Life and Times of John L. Sullivan, America's First Sports Hero*, Lyon's Press, Guilford, Conn., 2013.

Leonard, Sugar Ray, with Michael Arkush, *The Big Fight*, Viking Books, 2011.

Louis, Joe, with Edna and Art Rust Jr., *Joe Louis: My Life*, Harcourt Brace Jovanovich, New York and London, 1978.

Moore, Archie, with Leonard B. Pearl, *Any Boy Can, The Archie Moore Story*, Prentice Hall, 1971.

Paxton, Bill, *The Fearless Harry Greb*, McFarland & Company, Inc. Jefferson, North Carolina, 2009.

Remnick, David, *King of the World*, Random House, New York, 1999.

Roberts, Randy, *Jack Dempsey, The Manassa Mauler*, Louisiana State University Press, 1979.

Roberts, Randy, *Papa Jack, Jack Johnson and the Era of White Hopes*, The Free Press, New York, 1983.

Rudd, Irving, with Stan Fischler, *The Sporting Life*, St. Martin's Press, New York, 1990.

Schulberg, Budd, *Ringside, A Treasury of Boxing Reportage*, Ivan R. Dee, Chicago, 2006.

Sugar, Bert, *Bert Sugar on Boxing*, Lyons Press, Guilford, Conn., 2003.

Sugar, Bert, *Boxing's Greatest Fighters,* Lyons Press, Guilford, Conn., 2006.

Sullivan, Russell, *Rocky Marciano, The Rock of his Times,* University of Illinois Press, 2002.

Walker, Mickey, with Joe Reichler, *Mickey Walker, The Toy Bulldog & His Times,* Random House, New York, 1961.

Magazines and websites

Boxing Illustrated

GQ

Playboy

The Ring

Sport

Sports Illustrated

ESPN.com

Newspapers and newswire services

Associated Press

Brooklyn Daily Eagle

Brooklyn Standard Union

Buffalo Courier Express

Dayton Daily News

Detroit Free Press

Los Angeles Evening Citizen News

Los Angeles Times

Louisville Courier-Journal

Miami News

New London, The Day

New York Daily News

New York Newsday

New York Times

New York Tribune

New York World-Telegram and Sun

North American Newspaper Alliance

Philadelphia Daily News

Pittsburgh Post

Rochester Democrat and Chronicle

Sacramento Union

San Francisco Bulletin

Santa Rosa Press Democrat

St. Louis Post Dispatch

Tacoma Daily Register

Tacoma News Tribune

Toronto Star

United Press

Yonkers, Herald Statesman

Jack Newfield's quote about Ray Robinson is from the 1998 HBO special, *Sugar Ray Robinson: The Bright Lights and Dark Shadows of a Champion.*

Statistics

Historians are constantly adjusting the records of old-time fighters, which means different sources provide different numbers. This can be confusing for a general readership. In most cases, statistics for this book were culled from the International Boxing Hall of Fame Registry and website. – D.S.

About the Author

Don Stradley is a longtime contributor to *The Ring* magazine, with more than 20 years' experience in covering boxing. Born on a U.S. air base in the Azores, he is also a member of the Boxing Writers Association of America, having been cited many times for their annual awards, including top honors for News Story and Live Event coverage. He's also written for publications in the United Kingdom and South Africa, as well as for ESPN.com. He is the author of several books, most of them boxing related, including *The War*, a retrospective of the famous Hagler–Hearns bout, and *Berserk*, a biography of Edwin Valero.

𝕏 @DonStradley

ohn L. Sullivan · Jack Johnson · Har
reb · Jack Dempsey · Benny Leonard
Henry Armstrong · Archie Moore ·
oe Louis · Sugar Ray Robinson · Will
ep · Rocky Marciano · Muhammad Al
George Foreman · Sugar Ray Leonar
Mike Tyson · John L. Sullivan · Jack
ohnson · Harry Greb · Jack Dempsey
Benny Leonard · Henry Armstrong ·
rchie Moore · Joe Louis · Sugar Ray
obinson · Willie Pep · Rocky Marcia
Muhammad Ali · George Foreman ·
ugar Ray Leonard ·Mike Tyson · John
Sullivan · Jack Johnson · Harry Gr
Jack Dempsey · Benny Leonard · Hen
rmstrong · Archie Moore · Joe Loui
ugar Ray Robinson · Willie Pep · Roc
arciano · Muhammad Ali · George
oreman · Sugar Ray Leonard ·Mike T
John L. Sullivan · Jack Johnson · Ha
reb · Jack Dempsey · Benny Leonard

OHN L. SULLIVAN · JACK JOHNSON · HAR
IENRY ARMSTRONG · ARCHIE MOORE · JO
ROCKY MARCIANO · MUHAMMAD ALI · G
YSON · JOHN L. SULLIVAN · JACK JOHNSO
EONARD · HENRY ARMSTRONG · ARCHIE
WILLIE PEP · ROCKY MARCIANO · MUHA
EONARD · MIKE TYSON · JOHN L. SULLIVA
DEMPSEY · BENNY LEONARD · HENRY ARM
AY ROBINSON · WILLIE PEP · ROCKY MAR
SUGAR RAY LEONARD · MIKE TYSON · JOH
JACK DEMPSEY · BENNY LEONARD · HEN
SUGAR RAY ROBINSON · WILLIE PEP · RO
OREMAN · SUGAR RAY LEONARD · MIKE TY
IARRY GREB · JACK DEMPSEY · BENNY LEO
JOE LOUIS · SUGAR RAY ROBINSON · WIL
LI · GEORGE FOREMAN · SUGAR RAY LEO
OHNSON · HARRY GREB · JACK DEMPSEY
RCHIE MOORE · JOE LOUIS · SUGAR RAY
MUHAMMAD ALI · GEORGE FOREMAN · S
ULLIVAN · JACK JOHNSON · HARRY GREB
RMSTRONG · ARCHIE MOORE · JOE LOUIS